Murder
and
Redemption
at a
Benedictine
Abbey

Peace,
Paul Johnson

Paul Johnson

Murder and Redemption at a Benedictine Abbey.
Copyright © 2010 by Paul Richard Johnson.
All rights reserved. No part of this book may be used or
reproduced in any manner whatsoever without
written permission from the author except in
the case of brief quotations embodied in
critical articles or reviews.

ISBN: 1463573278
ISBN-13: 9781463573270

For the monks of Conception Abbey:
"I was a stranger and you welcomed me."
--The Rule of St. Benedict

Contents

✢ ✢ ✢

Introduction: A Question of Faith..... vii
Chapter One: Signs................1
Chapter Two: Fathers and Sons 11
Chapter Three: Catholics 29
Chapter Four: Telling Stories.......... 41
Chapter Five: Communion............. 49
Chapter Six: Brothers in Black........ 61
Chapter Seven: Crooked Lines......... 71
Chapter Eight: Euthyphro 81
Chapter Nine: The Woods 89
Chapter Ten: The Stranger............ 97
Chapter Eleven: Passages 107
Chapter Twelve: The Maze........... 123
Epilogue.......................... 129
Acknowledgments.................... 133
Notes............................. 135

INTRODUCTION:
A QUESTION OF FAITH

✤ ✤ ✤

I am here each time the stranger comes. He arrives like an accidental pilgrim would, turning in from the highway, drawn perhaps by the sight of the basilica towers or the sign on the highway: "Conception Abbey: Benedictine Monks." I have heard stories of people dropping in here for a day and staying for months. This man's visit today, however, is no accident.

For strangers and friends alike, the doors here are always open. So he enters the vestibule of the basilica. He's elderly and thin, dressed in a dark shirt and pants, with a Kansas City Royals baseball cap on his head. In his hands are two cardboard boxes. He puts these down on a wooden table in the vestibule and from them takes out two rifles: a coal-black MAK 90 and a Ruger .22 rifle with no stock. That's how they will be later identified in the police report. In my mind they are just rifles.

The Ruger he slings over his shoulder; the MAK 90 he carries in his hands.

He enters the nave of the basilica. I can't help wondering what thoughts are moving through his mind. What does a man think about here on the brink of what he is about to do? Is there a clear purpose, or only a confused jumble of disconnected thought along the frayed edge of madness? I can't answer these questions. No one can.

It's quiet in the basilica. The last Office, the set of daily prayers, was at seven and mass will not begin for a couple of hours. Father Timothy Schoen, who would normally be practicing the organ at this time, is away from the abbey this week. Bearing his guns, the stranger walks up the south side of the nave. He's headed for the door that leads into the monastery.

I am watching him from where I stand, in front near the altar. Sometimes I imagine myself in other places on this morning: On the road from Kearney, near Kansas City, where the stranger lives; out in the abbey parking lot where he parks his green Chevy Cavalier; in the vestibule when he enters. Or in the basilica itself, where I rush him before he can use his gun to stop me. It's a Hollywood fight, and the good guy always wins. I knock him down on the hard stone of the basilica floor and tear the MAK 90 out of his hands. Holding it by the barrel I swing the butt as hard as I can into the side of his head, staining the floor of the church with his blood. It is a sacrilege, here in this holy place, but I feel no remorse.

Today the dream is different. Today I don't attack him. Instead, I rush into the monastery to warn the monks. From the Glass Hallway, as the monks call it because of its many windows, connecting the basilica to the rest of the monastic cloister, I see Br. Damian. He is in the monastery courtyard, a grassy garden space enclosed by the square of the cloister.

He's smoking a pipe and looks up as I come out the from the monastery door, the one he will walk back through a minute from now. He will climb the stairs into the south hallway where he will be shot to death.

Br. Damian wants to show me how the flowers are growing in the courtyard. He takes care of the abbey grounds. He also watches the weather. People in the area know him as the Weather Monk. I know him for his smile and wave, usually from his seat on the tractor that he uses to mow the extensive lawns surrounding the abbey. He's always smoking a pipe. Like a farmer, he's at home around both machines and growing things. He loves watching storms.

I want to tell Br. Damian to stay out of the hallway, to hide, but that's impossible. In the strange impotence of dreams, I can't speak.

Taking the pipe from his mouth, Br. Damian smiles at me. He has the rough, weathered face of someone who spends a lot of time outdoors.

"How are those trains running?" I hear him ask me in his thick, rough voice.

Years ago I had built a model railroad in my basement. Occasionally, Br. Damian and I would talk about it. He said he had built one, too, when he was young. He talked about building one again, if he could find a place in the monastery to house it. For a man who struggles with depression like he does, it would make the winter days go easier for him.

"Well, I'm about done here," he says, more to himself than to me.

In the way of dreams I am back in the hallway, moving, running, but always too slowly. I am heading west, circling the square of the monastic cloister, all the way around to the porter's office, which is next to the foyer and the front door of the monastery. Fr. Philip is there, as I know he will be. Like Br. Damian, he smiles when he sees me, and rises from his seat. "Have you come back to stay with us?" I hear him say. When I stayed in the monastery some years back, it was Fr. Philip who greeted me at the front door.

Then I hear the sound of the first rifle shots. They're very loud, even here on the other side of the cloister. They echo down the long, wooden-floored hallway, a sound that's never been heard in here before. Soon there are more. Fr. Philip leaves, but not to run away. Instead, he turns down the hallway *toward* the shots. A few seconds later, I hear the sound of two more shots, then silence. I stand waiting, seeing everything, yet unable to save them, unable to change what has already happened.

Then I am again in the basilica, at the back this time. It's so quiet, I can almost hear the faint sound of sirens coming from the west. I see the stranger. He's slumped over in one of the back pews as if he'd fallen asleep. I smell the burned powder from the final bullet. It hangs in the air like incense. There's a pool of blood on the floor beneath the pew.

My eyes find their way up the nave toward the altar and to the ceiling above and beyond it. Mary is pictured there, enthroned amid the stars. My mouth is moving. It may be a prayer, but it could be that I am merely mumbling wordless questions into the silence. Perhaps, after all, there is no difference.

Such dreams and fantasies of intervention played over and over again in my head in the weeks after June 10th of 2002. But they were only that: pathetic and impotent desires, prompted by loss. I was not at Conception Abbey when Lloyd Jeffress arrived with his two rifles. That morning I was in Maryville, the town where I live, fifteen miles away.

Yet I kept imagining myself there, either as a helpless spectator or a blessed savior, stepping in to stop the deaths of Br. Damian Larsen and Fr. Philip Schuster. I would do what God didn't do—what he chose not to do, because, as the religious philosophers argue, that's the kind of world he made: People in our world are free to love, and free to kill.

Small consolation.

Small god.

So I believed at the time, and so the thought sometimes returns to trouble me nearly a decade after the shootings at Conception Abbey, especially when I hear news of other madmen killing other innocents.

The shootings came at a time in my life when I was struggling with my trust and faith in God. At that time I had been working for the monks of Conception Abbey for twelve years as a teacher of English in their seminary college. I had been a Christian for twenty-eight years.

Conception Seminary College has existed here in various forms since 1886, when the first abbot of Conception, Frowin Conrad, founded it. Education has always been a central work of the Benedictine order and the four-year liberal arts seminary remains the chief apostolic mission of the abbey. This place is different, however, than Catholic colleges in this region of the country, such as Rockhurst in Kansas City or Benedictine College in Atchison. Young men come to Conception to receive a college education, but the main focus of their years at the seminary is on formation for the Catholic priesthood. This is a place where faith matters.

I had known that from the start. I could remember sitting in Brother Thomas Sullivan's office early in my interview for a job at the seminary. Br. Thomas was Academic Dean of the college at that time.

"Do you have faith?" he asked me.

Did I have faith? Answering the question, for me, was complicated. I was Protestant. I had converted to Christianity in high school, adopting a relatively conservative Evangelicalism that prided itself on being confident about the big questions of life. This confidence continued through my college years until graduate school, where it was eroded by many increasingly disturbing questions: How do we "have" faith? Is it like something we own, or is it a condition? Is faith a thing or an event? A noun or a verb? An answer, or a question that is never answered, never settled? Is faith a refuge of certainty, or a crucible of doubt?

But I judged that a job interview at a Catholic seminary college wasn't the place to get into questions like these. The monks needed an answer and I needed the job. "I have faith," I said simply.

Later, I was interviewed by Fr. Gregory Polan, then the President-Rector of the college. He asked me much the same question. I remember telling him that he didn't have to worry about my faith. More than anything, I wanted to reassure him. Questions of how a Protestant would fit into the peculiar religious culture of a Benedictine abbey would, I thought, take care of themselves. The rest of the interview went well and the following week the monks hired me.

So it was that three months later, with my wife and eight-month old son, I came to Conception in a diesel-powered U-Haul truck on the day that Saddam Hussein invaded Kuwait. We heard about it on the radio. Momentous things were happening in the larger world outside. Our lives and future were changing, too. We were leaving Madison, Wisconsin, a beautiful, bustling, progressive city we had loved, and driving to Maryville, a small Missouri town on the edge of the Great Plains. I wasn't sorry to be done with graduate school, but we were leaving behind friends and moving to a strange place where we knew no one, and to a job at a Benedictine abbey in the middle of nowhere.

In the years to come, the question of my faith gradually disappeared. At least, I stopped thinking about it very much. I settled comfortably into teaching at Conception Seminary College. My wife Carolyn and I joined the local Episcopal congregation, raised our son and gradually got adjusted to living in Maryville. Life became an enjoyable, predictable routine. In my job at the abbey, I was surrounded by people of faith. I liked them; they liked me. The years passed.

In late June of 2001 this comfortable routine was disturbed by my brother's death. Ten years earlier Kurt had been diagnosed HIV positive. Coming to terms with this revelation about both his life and impending death began to change many things in my life: my prejudices about homosexuality; my comfortable certainties about faith. I wasn't fully aware of the change until the loss and grief that had been put on ice for a decade came back to life in an intensive care unit in Minneapolis. With medication Kurt had outpaced AIDS but succumbed to a sudden pancreatic infection. There was no hope of recovery. After my family decided to have him removed from life support, I watched my brother die.

Kurt was forty. Considered in the abstract, his death was no special case. Many die before their time, as we like to imagine what their "time" should be. It happens every hour and minute and second of every day. And I had faced early death in my family before: My father had died relatively young. That had been a difficult time, too, but I had gotten over it. I would get over this, I thought, and life would go on as it always had.

But something happened to me during that following year. Death had come close, so close that I could smell its bitter breath. All the old questions about life, death, and faith returned.

Do you have faith? Br. Thomas had asked me all those years ago. I had answered yes to him then; now, I wasn't so sure.

All those feelings I had felt, all the pious acts I had performed, all the books I had read and believed, all the arguments I had made—they now seemed only the empty gestures of fear and delusion. The God I had trusted—or thought I had trusted—was silent, as he always had been, except that now the silence seemed like a cold, wintry vacancy.

This hit me hard one Sunday morning as I sat in church. That morning everything seemed to collapse inward, like a fading star imploding into a black hole, until only blank nothingness remained. The wood and plaster and robes and other accouterments of liturgy were emptied of significance. At the same time I could hear a voice in my head speaking in silent descant with the prayers of the people around me: *Do you really believe in this Paul?*

A few months later came the shootings. That day was like our own 9/11. It thrust into the very heart of this place of peace the sharp terror of indiscriminate slaughter. But the terrorism of September 11th, at least, had a motive; June 10th had none that we could ever know. Death came at random: Whoever happened to be in the hallway of the monastery that morning when Lloyd Jeffress walked through was shot, and the stranger took his reasons to the grave.

A Question of Faith

Human beings tell stories to make sense of how things go in the world. It is a way for us to find some kind of meaning in human existence. As an English teacher, stories have been my life: I had loved reading them in my youth, been trained how to interpret them in college, and had come to Conception Abbey to teach them to Catholic seminarians.

However, the murder of Brother Damian Larsen and Father Philip Schuster was a story beyond my skill to understand. It had no plot, only event, like some fragmented, absurd, postmodern narrative. And if there was any good to be had from it, any higher purpose to be discerned, to me the cost seemed very high. Where in this could faith find purchase? All I had, it seemed, were unanswerable questions in a bleak, God-haunted world.

But I was wrong. As I would come to see in time, I also had the monks. For two decades these men in black have been my faithful, patient friends and fellow-travelers in a world of enigmas. Despite what had happened on June 10th and the questions they all carried—and still carry—about what it meant, they did not lose faith. The monks bore witness to a greater hope. Through their lives, God called me back.

This book is about that journey of faith, even when the journey didn't look like faith at all. It's about my life as both teacher and learner, believer and doubter at Conception Abbey, a place of peace touched by insane evil. It's about the monks and students who live, work, and study here and what they have taught me about faith. It is not an easy story for me to tell, but I am encouraged by the hope that there may be others out there like me who have lived with questions, doubt, or even the loss of their faith, broken by crisis or thinned away through boredom or neglect.

I offer no radical insights here into either the Benedictine way of life or Catholic seminary education. What I do offer is a testimony, a witness, as I might have said in my evangelical years. Back then I believed that Catholics needed to be saved because they weren't born again; now I see how much my own salvation has been nurtured by Catholics, even before I understood what Catholicism was. Faith, I have learned, is a journey rather than a destination, and a difficult, stumbling journey at that. For half my Christian life that journey has been made with the students and monks of Conception Abbey.

Over my years at the abbey I have become, as one of my former students put it, an insider/outsider. I am a part of this place and its apostolic ministry of priestly formation. I am also separate—even alienated at times—because of who I am: a Protestant among Catholics, and one who continues to wrestle with the deep questions of faith.

Yet if there is any place where the pilgrim can find rest and soul-food for the journey, it is here. At a time when polarization seems to be the condition of life in this country and religion has for many become synonymous with hatred, violence, abuse, and political expediency, I have experienced something quite different with the monks of Conception: welcome for the stranger. This simple ethic is a way of life for Benedictine monks, and has been for a millennium and a half. It applies to any stranger, even the one who comes with two rifles, bent on murder. The doors of Conception Abbey were open for Robert Lloyd Jeffress on June 10th. They remain open today.

CHAPTER ONE:
SIGNS

✤ ✤ ✤

This is, perhaps, one of the deserts of our world. Northwest Missouri may look that way to the person moving in the speed-dial, broadband lanes of life, one of those fly-over places that you glimpse from the window of an airplane on a clear day and wonder, "who would want to live there?"—then let out a thankful sigh that you don't.

That may be an advantage for the seeker. Walker Percy wrote that in our time the "survivor of theory and consumption becomes a wayfarer in the desert, like St. Anthony: which is to say, open to signs."[1] And deserts, even when they're not really deserts but rolling, rich farmland, can be places of discernment and transformation for those with ears open to God's subtle voice. Conception Abbey has been that kind of place for pilgrims and oblates on retreat, for students coming to study at the seminary, or for would-be monks joining the monastery.

For me, it's a job. And if God is speaking to me today, it's in the weight of the daily, the everyday life that I live. That's what I carry now, on my way to work, traveling south on Route #71 from Maryville on an ordinary Monday morning a couple of weeks after the start of the fall semester. It's mostly professional: I'm thinking about my upcoming classes and the other tasks that need to get done today: There are papers to grade and classes to prepare, the usual labor of teaching.

Even though I've traveled this road hundreds of times, I still watch for signs. The first one appears on the side of the road five miles south of Maryville. It's a letter U, with an arrow pointing east. Here I turn down a county road of cracked and pitted asphalt. In this part of the state the grain of the land runs from north to south, so the road dips and rises and dips again, between steep ridges climbing out of little wooded valleys with their clay-dark creeks that amble south toward the Missouri River.

In less than a mile, the hills flatten out into a broad river valley covered with wide fields of corn and soybean. There's little traffic as I move through the tiny hamlet of Arkoe, hard by the Hundred and Two River, once an important railroad stop on the Burlington between Kansas City and Council Bluffs. Beyond are more ridges to climb.

I've never grown tired of this road. It presents a tableau of change in constancy—the fields, the colors of leaf and grain, the weather of the day, all changing, passing with the seasons over the everlasting hills and valleys. This is a country I've grown used to. It isn't home to me, though, even after almost two decades of living here. My heart's home is in the north, amid the deep forests, clear lakes, and rocky hills of northeast Minnesota. I used to feel like an exile, a sojourner in a land that was altogether too warm for most of the year. But over the years the land and its people have grown on me.

As my car crests each hill and the wide Missouri sky opens around me, I am praying. The twenty-minute drive from Maryville gives me space and time for this, when I choose. This morning I'm feeling numb and distracted and my prayers are sketchy, short. I keep at it, remembering what the monks have taught me, that prayer is something we choose to do no matter what our feelings of the moment. It is a discipline rather than an aesthetic.

I didn't always understand prayer this way. In my early spiritual life, I was continually bouncing between poles of piety and boredom, depending upon my mood. I was young and needy, embracing intense new devotions, then growing tired of them within weeks. I believe now that most practices of piety never suited me for long because I was using them to please someone else by trying to be someone else. So if I rose at five in the morning and had devotions for an hour, prayed extra hard and long, I would make myself worthy of God's love, like I believed I needed to make myself worthy of my father's love.

I still fall into this habit of appeasement from time to time and I'm still no more successful at devotional pieties than I used to be. They tend to keep me too deep inside my own head, the interior closet, to paraphrase St. Teresa of Avila. With my introverted, ruminating personality, that's a dangerous place to be.

What saves me is simplicity: In my prayer life I keep returning to a simple surrendering of my life to God in the face of what might lie ahead of me on any particular day. Some days the surrender is easy and natural, like the satisfaction of sexual longing, only larger and less purely physical. I feel it as a hollowness inside my chest, a soulful emptiness that must be filled and refilled often. This is what prayer has become for me: an opening to love.

Then there are those days when I feel nothing at all and discipline wanes. My way is just an ordinary country road between ripening fields, and prayer is a movement of the lips, but without thought—or life. Like this morning, as my car climbs heavily over the hills. Prayer seems an impossible struggle. Doubt hovers close, a malaise like a vague ache in the bones. This morning I'm feeling the weight of my life. It must be Monday.

"I can't carry this alone," I say aloud, to the windshield, beyond which the empty road, like time itself, is rushing toward me, past me. A few seconds later I mutter, "I believe; help my unbelief." It's the prayer of the father of the epileptic boy in the ninth chapter of the gospel of Mark, and I often find myself using it. It expresses my difficulties with trusting God, yet still wanting to. Sometimes, when everything else seems broken, all I've got left is the desire for God.

Meanwhile, the car finds its way, over the final miles of this ragged patchwork of a road, across the Platte River valley and up the last ridge toward Conception Abbey, where the two towers of the basilica rise from the trees. In my prayer there is no resolution, only a vague trailing off from sentences into fragments and then single words of need and desire accompanied by a sense of unfinished business, and a subtle urge to leave things open. I don't know where this thought comes from. It seems good and right and I want to believe that it's God voice, but it could just be me and for all I know, it's both.

At the top of the hill I pass through part of the village of Conception and turn into the abbey parking lot and on past the west front of the basilica. Built of red brick, with a solid, simple, Romanesque design, the church is made to withstand the fierce winds that blow through this country. In two niches over the doors of the west portal are winged statues of angels, Gabriel and Michael. One of Michael's wings is missing.

Joined to the south side of the basilica is the monastery. Its solid, four-story walls are topped by a steep copper roof, oxidized to the color of slate. Though to modern eyes the monastery may look like a fortress to keep out the world, it's designed as a sanctuary of prayer and peace. The basilica, with the cloister to the south, forms the core of the monastery, in which the monks live. Outside of this are the other abbey buildings: lodgings for pilgrims and guests, workshops, and, of course, the seminary where I work.

"Why here?" A friend of mine once asked me when I showed him a postcard with a panoramic aerial photograph of Conception Abbey. It was a good question. How did there come to be a monastery here on this windy ridge, miles from anywhere?

The history of Conception Abbey began in Reading, Pennsylvania, and Engelberg, Switzerland. In 1858, because of economic hardship and bleak prospects for the future, Irish Catholic laborers moved from Reading to farm land near what is now the town of Conception. German farmers from southern Missouri later joined the Irish colony, desiring to escape the slavery of southern Missouri. They wanted priests who could preach and hear their confessions in German.

Enter: the monks. Following the Civil War, the Abbey of Engelberg, in Switzerland, became entwined in the life of the Irish colonists of Conception. Threatened with the suppression of their abbey by the Swiss government, Abbot Anselm of Engelberg sent two Benedictine monks to America to found an abbey as a possible asylum. Through several contacts they came to Northwest Missouri to assist the spiritual needs of the colonists near Conception. New Engelberg Abbey of the Immaculate

Conception was founded in 1873 and renamed Conception Abbey in 1891 when the new abbey church was dedicated.

I remember the first time I ever came here. It was in the spring of 1990 and I was completing graduate school at the University of Wisconsin. All winter I had scoured the job ads in *The Chronicle of Higher Education*. I applied to every position for which I was remotely qualified, including one for an English teacher at a small Catholic seminary college named Conception, in Missouri.

One day I got a call. The monks were interested in hiring me. Could I come down for an interview?

I liked the idea of teaching at a small college like Conception, but I had some reservations: The starting salary was low and the college so isolated I couldn't even find the town of Conception in our road atlas. I did locate "Conception Junction"—a suggestively fertile name if there ever was one—in the northwestern corner of Missouri. Conception Abbey had to be close by. If so, it was at least a hundred miles from any major city. Also, it was a Catholic seminary, and I was Protestant. Well, I thought, if they were interested in me I'd go and take a look. Besides, I didn't have a lot of other choices.

The first sign that I might have found something good at Conception came before the day of interviews had even started. At around seven in the morning I was awakened by the sound of bells ringing. I read on the information card in my room that the second prayer office of the day, called "lauds," was about to begin.

I knew about the monastic hours of prayer from reading *The Name of the Rose* and I had grown up with the sound of church bells, but they were recorded ones playing from speakers mounted in the spire of Queen of Peace Catholic Church on the hill above our house. The bells of Conception Abbey were real, rung by real monks. Their sound made me feel like I had been transported from the age of television and computers to an older world where mystery and holiness wore a palpable shape. It was strangely attractive to me and I remembered thinking that I could be happy working here.

A couple of weeks later, after I had returned to school in Madison and accepted the job offer the monks had made, I remembered the books. They were still on a shelf back in the closet of the room that doubled as a nursery and office in our tiny Eagle Heights apartment: an old Everyman's Library edition of John Ruskin's three-volume work on gothic architecture, *The Stones of Venice*. I had bought them a year before in a bookstore on State Street in Madison. I was interested in Ruskin, one of the most important and popular English writers of the nineteenth century, but mostly I had been intrigued by the previous owner's name inscribed in pencil inside the front cover: *Frater Conrad, Conception Abbey*.

At the time, I realized that the books had been owned by a monk: I didn't know Latin, but *Frater* looked like *fraternal* or *fraternity*—another way to say brother, I thought. My impression was of something archaic and cryptic and holy, especially when connected to the word *abbey*. It appealed to my romantic side, as well as my new-found love of Anglican sacrament and liturgy in the Episcopal Church.

I bought the books, but because I had so many others to read at the time, they went onto my shelf and were forgotten. Until now. I dug them out and took them in to show our graduate advisor, Donald Rowe, a medievalist with a Chaucerian sense of humor. "It's a sign," he said with an ironic chuckle.

After I began working at Conception Abbey, I sought out Frater Conrad. At that time Conrad Falk—Father, now—had been a monk for nearly fifty years and a priest for almost forty. He had taught philosophy and logic and served as both academic dean and president of the seminary. Now, in his seventies, he was working in the Abbey Business Office. I introduced myself, then held out one of the Ruskin books to him with the front cover opened to his name.

"Father, do you remember this book?"

He took it in his hands, looking at the name, then at me. His face was molded in solid, square lines, his eyes clear and questioning.

"I'm not sure," he said slowly, looking down again at the inscription. "I must have bought them when I was in Rome."

Fr. Conrad had gone to Rome in 1949 to study theology in preparation for ordination to the priesthood. Years later, he told me, he had given the Ruskin books to the abbey librarian, who later sold them on the used book market. They wound up in a book shop in Madison, eventually finding their way to me, a year before I'd applied for the job at Conception.

With a faint smile, Fr. Conrad closed the book and handed it back to me.

Though I have never taken it as much more than an extraordinary coincidence, there are times when I can't help wondering if my discovery of Fr. Conrad's books in a bookstore in Madison was a sign, as Don Rowe had humorously suggested. If so, of what? By definition, signs signify; they say something. However, this one was ambiguous at best. Had God planned my way, chosen my job, given me an "invitation" by planting the name of Conception Abbey in my mind so I would apply for the position?

I don't know. I've never been much of a believer in signs and wonders. Back in college I knew people who claimed that God regularly showed them signs and sometimes even talked to them directly. He never talked to me and I was always pretty glad of it. I used to imagine what it would have been like to be sitting in my dorm room and suddenly hear God's voice booming out of my stereo speakers; afterward, staggering into the hallway, my hair turned white like Charlton Heston's in *The Ten Commandments* as he came down from Sinai.

The story about Fr. Conrad's books got around the monastery. With their usual equanimity, the monks accepted it as one of those strange twists of circumstance: They aren't much for wacky signs or pious drivel.

After Fr. Conrad died of acute leukemia in 1998, I tucked the death notice with his picture and obituary into one of the books that he once owned and which came to me, a stranger, and yet a distant spiritual brother, too. I keep them as a memorial and a reminder that, as Frederick Buechner says, there is "no chance thing through which God cannot speak."[2]

Chapter Two:
Fathers and Sons

✤ ✤ ✤

The Road has brought me to my office in St. Benedict Hall. It's an old dorm room on the ground floor crammed to the ceiling with books—about six shelves of them, with more stuffed into the closets. I unlock the door and switch on the lights, pouring a cup of coffee from the thermos I've brought from home. A few minutes later a monk looks in through my open door.

Father Kenneth Reichert is on his way to his office just down the hall. This morning he's wearing a dark blue jacket over his Benedictine habit and blue baseball cap tilted back on his head with the words "Fort Worth Stockyards" embossed on the front. He says hello and we have a few words about the weather, which is unusually cool for this early in September. "Maybe it's going to snow tonight," he says with a hearty chuckle. I tell him that would be great. "But then," I add, "I'm from Minnesota."

Seeing Fr. Kenneth reminds me of the stability and steadiness of Benedictine life, the dedication to prayer and service without fanfare. He is both a spiritual director for the students and prior of the monastery, in charge of things when the abbot is away. Saint Benedict, the founder of the order, didn't like the idea of having a prior because he felt there was too much opportunity for abuse of power. However, when I think of Fr. Kenneth Reichert, I imagine St. Benedict in heaven nodding his head with approval. Fr. Kenneth's spirituality, like that of the other monks, is rooted in prayer, a waiting and attentiveness that seeks inner silence, even as it remains firmly connected to daily reality.

I've known Fr. Kenneth for as long as I've worked at Conception: he was guestmaster when I first came here. He has taught me a great deal about faith, though I think he would be surprised to hear me say that. It isn't so much in what he says, but in how he lives and serves others. This is especially true since that day in June of 2002 when he and Fr Norbert Schappler were nearly shot to death in the monastery by a man they had never met before.

Fr. Kenneth leaves just as Dr. John Bloomingdale shows up at his office across the hall. John and I have been colleagues here at Conception for over fifteen years. Like me, he came here right out of graduate school. He's a psychologist, and we spend a few minutes talking about a course we're planning to teach next semester on post-modernism. Then I hurriedly gather my notes for the first class of the day, Writing I. It's made up of the new class of freshmen at Conception Seminary College.

As I leave my office, I catch up to Dr. Christopher Anadale, who teaches philosophy. This morning he's on his way to his course on epistemology. Together, we walk over to St. Maur Hall, the main classroom building, carrying on some easy, early-morning conversation. He tells me about a Web site he's discovered featuring philosopher action figures like Nietzsche, with "eternally recurring punch action."[1] I'll check it out later to leaven the day.

On our way we pass seminarians and a monk or two, who all greet us. Here, I know almost everyone and they know me, and that's a good feeling. I say hello to Fr. Donald Grabner, who has been a monk here since the late 1940's. He's one of the most well-read persons I've ever met, including most of the professors I had in graduate school. Fr. Donald's many interests range from Christology to comparative religion to the fiction of Flannery O'Connor. He's visited Tibetan monasteries in India and attended conferences in this country on the history of Islam. To me, he epitomizes the Catholic Church at its best: the missional church, embracing diversity, welcoming the stranger; listening, learning, not afraid of who or what it might encounter in the world.

Inside the front doors of St. Maur I look up into the vast open space of the rotunda, with its grand staircase angling up three floors. Each floor has a railed balcony overlooking the entrance. These have become favorite places for seminarians to stand and watch people coming in and out of the building. This morning I see three of them standing at the second floor railing. I'll call them Dmitri, Alyosha, and Ivan, characters from my favorite Russian novel.[2]

Ivan is standing nearest to me as I reach the top of the stairway. He is taller than me, with short brown hair and blue eyes, punctuated with a cleft chin. He gives me a nod and a quiet smile of greeting.

Unlike his namesake in Dostoevski's novel, my Ivan is not an atheist. But he is intelligent and has excelled in his courses at the seminary, including Fr. Isaac True's philosophy classes. This isn't easy to do: Fr. Isaac has a formidable reputation here.

I call him Ivan mostly because, like Dostoevski's character, he has a tendency to "live in his head"—to think and ruminate a lot. It's a trait that I share with him and ever since I got to know him last spring in my American Novel class, I have considered him a kindred spirit.

In my years of teaching literature in the seminary, I have found that for students to fully understand a work of art like a novel or short story, they must listen with a mind and heart attuned to the subtle, complex chords of character. There are relatively few students with this gift, but Ivan is one of them. It emerged in the class discussions we had on novels such as *The Sun Also Rises*, *Their Eyes Were Watching God*, and *The Second Coming*. I was especially impressed with the psychologically probing essays he wrote. Gradually over the semester he and I became friends. I got curious about where Ivan, an introvert, gained his insight into people and the emotional tendencies in character. One day last year, late in the spring, he and I sat down in my office to talk about that, and other things.

Ivan is a cradle Catholic and he served as an altar boy at Mass and funerals. Even in those early days, the possibility of becoming a priest was in his heart. As he grew older, though, Ivan drifted away from the Church. What brought him back, as it so often does, was a crisis in his personal life. It came after he had begun a major in electrical engineering at Iowa State University.

"Why engineering?" I asked him.

"To prove I could do it," he said with a wry smile. "Sounds pretty stupid and arrogant, doesn't it?"

Actually, it didn't sound stupid at all, only human—and very familiar to me: I'd done roughly the same thing at about the same age for the same reason. For me, it was an act rooted in both need and fear. Back then I thought I knew everything and was anxious to demonstrate that belief to others. Mastery of ideas gave me the illusion that I was in command of other parts of my life. I thought I knew who I was and what I wanted to become, like the brainy but crippled Hulga in Flannery O'Connor's short story, "Good Country People." It would take years for me to understand the truth about myself.

"At Iowa State I was paying out-of-state tuition and working two jobs to afford it," Ivan continued. "After a year I was doing so badly in school that they were going to kick me out if I didn't get my act together."

There were other issues in his life—long-standing ones he hadn't yet faced. While he waited to be re-admitted to college, Ivan spent weeks alone in his room in the apartment he was sharing with his sister. He was isolated, lonely, and depressed. "It was a very dark time," he said.

One day he found himself on the Iowa State campus with some time to kill so he went to the university library. For some reason the name of St. Augustine was in his mind that day, though he had never read anything by this fifth-century saint. Ivan looked up the name in the library catalog and randomly picked one of the titles he found there. After writing down the call number, he headed up to the philosophy section on the third floor of the library. As he came down one of the shelf-lined aisles he saw a book propped halfway off the shelf into the aisle, as if it were there waiting for him. He pulled the book out and looked at the title: It turned out to be St. Augustine's *Confessions*, and the call number was already written on the paper in his hand.

Ivan is generally not a believer in special signs from God, but this did seem like a strange coincidence to him. He checked the book out from the library. A month and a half later it still sat on his shelf, unread. By then he owned it—the book had been checked out so long the university made him purchase it.

He had failed out of the engineering program with no inkling of what he was going to do with the rest of his life. Though Ivan had a job, he was forced to sell his television and Sony Playstation for food and rent money. It seemed like he had hit bottom. With free time on his hands, in the desert of his own vulnerability and need, he picked up *Confessions* and began to read.

From the first page, the book enthralled him, as it has so many over the centuries. For Ivan, *Confessions* was familiar and compelling, the story of a saint who had struggled hard with dedicating his life to God, yet was willing to be transformed.

"Our hearts are restless until they rest in you," I said aloud, remembering the familiar quotation from the beginning of that work.

Ivan nodded: "The whole thing is a poem, a prayer—it's beautiful."

Reading *Confessions* moved Ivan to put a question to himself—the question of questions, and one that had been with him for a long time, since his childhood, in fact: *What do I want to do with my life? Do I want to be honest in what I believe is my relationship with God and dedicate myself to that—or not?* It was, and eventually Ivan entered Conception Seminary College, and ended up in my American literature class.

Like anything worth doing, the work of formation has been a challenge for him. Ivan had expectations when he came to Conception about how the school should be run and what the teachers should be like. "I was really arrogant," he confessed, and he had a lot to say about what he thought was wrong about the seminary. Was this the best place for him to dedicate himself to God? He wasn't sure.

What finally convinced him that it was worthwhile for him to submit himself to the process of priestly formation at Conception and face the reality of what was in his own heart was the day-to-day experience of living his faith within a community. He had never understood this before, even growing up in a Catholic family of eight children. Now he realized how antithetical and damaging his former isolation had been to living an authentic Christian life.

At Conception Ivan found, to his relief, that his fellow seminarians weren't a bunch of "praying robots," as he put it. They were all serious about what they were doing at the seminary, but they knew how to enjoy themselves, too. It was a revelation about the life he was being called to live, that it was situated firmly in reality—not only the reality of ideas, which he was well acquainted with, but also of persons and things. It was about love, self-sacrifice, and the discernment of beauty and meaning in the world.

A natural diplomat who empathizes with others' weakness, Ivan forged close friendships among seminarians with widely varying backgrounds and religious convictions. It seemed clear to me that there was a connection between his empathy and the skill with which he understood characters in stories. His own pain had become a doorway out of the closed room of his isolation and loneliness—but he was the one who had to open the door. Beyond it he discovered a wider, more generous country, where love could become the pathway to growth and freedom—and understanding.

Standing to Ivan's left, leaning over the railing, is Dmitri, a junior. He is shorter than Ivan by nearly a foot, with a broader, more muscular build. His face is full of good humor, with green eyes and a grin that makes you wonder what he's been up to.

I call him Dmitri, but he is not Dostoevski's brawling, reckless sensualist. Yet he is, as he characterizes himself, "ornery" (pronounced "ahnery")—he has a passionate and instinctive love of freedom and fun that pushes at limits and boundaries. But for all his air of *bon vivant*, Dmitri possesses a sober dedication to the discernment of his priestly vocation. I was interested in this apparent contradiction in him and a few days earlier he and I got to talking about his life and how he ended up at Conception.

Dmitri grew up in the same Wichita, Kansas parish all his life. He went to a Catholic high school and to Mass with his family every Sunday. He's always had a serious, thoughtful side to him, he told me, but in high school he was more serious about having a good time than living his Christian faith. Then the unexpected happened: his brother-in-law, a former student at Conception, asked Dmitri to consider attending the seminary.

It seemed unlikely to him—impossible, even—that a guy like him might be called to the priesthood, but he came up for a visit to Conception during the spring of his Senior year of high school. As Dmitri recalls, he expected to find "a bunch of pious, hand-waving guys" at the seminary; like Ivan before him, what he found was just the opposite: "They were like me, serious about being at the seminary, but also able to have a good time." The encounter convinced him to give the place a try, at least for a year.

That first semester at the seminary was a shock for him. "You come in here and think you've got everything figured out," Dmitri recalled. "That all you need is a little polishing up and you're ready for the priesthood. The longer you're here, though, the more you see how much you have to learn." He paused, then said with a grin, "You get a nice thick slab of humble pie."

The seminary assigns a chaplain to each class of seminarians. The chaplains live with the students in the dormitories. Their responsibility is the external forum, which is how student behavior might indicate deeper character issues that need addressing. Chaplains deal with anything from students missing classes and Mass, to more serious issues such as substance abuse. The chaplain plays multiple roles of gatekeeper, enforcer, counselor, reality instructor, and friend.

In his Freshman year, Dmitri's chaplain was Fr. Sebastian Allgaier, a former buck sergeant in the Air Force and a monk skilled at discerning and uncovering character flaws that might hinder the process of priestly formation. Among the students there was a saying about Fr. Sebastian's approach to formation, as Dmitri explained: "At first you think he's over the edge. Then you hate him. By the end of the second semester you respect him. By the next year you wish you had him back as a chaplain."

Dmitri's own appreciation of Fr. Sebastian would come eventually, but he had a lot of work to do first. Through frank, sometimes confrontational, conversations, Fr. Sebastian pushed Dmitri to look at himself clearly and honestly. It wasn't easy for him and the seminarian began to resent it. One day when he and some other seminarians were at a bowling alley in town, Dmitri started complaining about his chaplain. An older seminarian sat him down—hard: "Man-up and get a grip," he said.

"The Church is taking teenagers fresh out of high school and in eight years making them caretakers of people's souls. They need to get into every nook and cranny of your life. They need to know—and you need to know—that you're serious about this." Dmitri didn't take this advice well at first. He wondered if it was all worth the pain. There seemed to be too many people telling him how to live.

There was another reason to doubt his choice of seminary, a young woman back home who Dmitri had known since elementary school. I'll call her Katerina. The two of them were close friends, and that friendship had deepened in the months before he came to Conception. He couldn't keep seeing her, of course, and remain in the seminary. That was the rule. But he couldn't stop thinking about her, either, especially in the midst of his struggles with Fr. Sebastian. Katerina seemed to offer the possibility of a life altogether different than the one he had embarked on. Questions tread-milled in his head: *Was this relationship serious? If he played the game with her, would it be for something—or nothing? Should he leave the seminary?*

After a couple of weeks of this, as November came with its winter-browns and grays, he couldn't stand it any longer and told his spiritual director about Katerina. Spiritual direction in the seminary is based upon the ancient monastic practice of seeking out an elder for guidance in how to live one's life under the gaze of God. Dmitri's spiritual director advised him that if he was serious about the priesthood, he needed to cut off the relationship. He did it over the phone, and Katerina understood, knowing Dmitri and why he was in the seminary.

That would have been it, except that Dmitri couldn't resist a last lingering glance back at what might have been. It was dangerous, but he wanted to know, so he asked Katerina how she felt about him. It was a tempting emotional game to play as a seminarian, Dmitri told me, to see if you still "had it"—could still charm a woman, even make her regret that you were in the seminary. He knew at the time it was wrong, but still he asked.

"I wouldn't want to marry you," she said. "But I know you're someone I could talk to when I'm having problems."

Her words felt like a knife-stab. It hurt. Dmitri wanted to be wanted, even if he was only playing with the idea. That was his first reaction. The second was ecstasy. He realized, despite his own emotional confusion, that Katerina had confirmed what Dmitri had only begun to see in himself: that the seminary was the right place for him to be at this point in his life.

A year and a half went by before he saw her again. This past summer they were able to reconnect as the good friends they used to be, to talk together without the expectations that had tripped them up before. Katerina's friendship has helped convince Dmitry that celibacy is a gift rather than a denial or an exclusion.

This isn't easily understood by people he meets outside the seminary: Once, when Dmitri was in a Starbuck's back home drinking coffee with his best friend in the seminary, someone asked them where they went to college. A Catholic seminary, they answered.

"Is that, like, a 'you-can't-have-sex school' or something? How can you deal with that?"

Dmitri laughed when he told me this, then wondered aloud how college students deal with living at a secular university without the kind of standards that have guided and formed his life over the past two years at the seminary. They are very different academic worlds, to be sure, and there is no doubt that had he attended Kansas State, Dmitri's life would have gone much differently than it has. Seminary formation has helped him mature in ways he couldn't have imagined, once he accepted what

Fr. Sebastian was telling him about himself. Before you can minister to people, Dmitri has learned, you have to be able to take care of yourself; to take care of yourself, you have to understand yourself.

Dmitri's sophomore year brought a key moment of self-understanding: a realization that discernment about the priesthood was not based on emotions. Some days, with homework piling up and other things falling apart, he didn't want to be at the seminary, but he learned to look past these passing troubles and stress. "How I feel isn't a measure of how I'm doing here," he said with a serious, thoughtful tone. It was an essential realization, rare in someone Dmitri's age, and I admired him for it.

He also discovered how much the support and respect of his peers—his brother seminarians—meant to him, even more than the approval of his superiors. He's never doubted that the seminary has had his best in mind, but his peers have given him the most effective criticism. "When one of your brothers tells you you're screwing up," Dmitri said, "It means a lot more."

Over the past two years Dmitri has become more serious, working hard to shed the "class clown" reputation he had earned as a Freshman, but he hasn't lost touch with his "ornery" side. "It's part of who I am," he said. "By the end of Freshman year I wanted to grow out of immaturity. This year," he adds with a grin, "I want to embrace my 'true Dmitri-ness.'"

I laughed, telling him that I was glad. I've known a number of "Dmitris" in my years at the seminary. They liven things up in the classroom, and their spirit among the seminarians has generated some memorable campus pranks, like removing the furniture, books, clothing—everything—out of a seminarian's room and attaching a forged note from the seminary administration informing him that he had been expelled. Or dismantling the Abbey Center golf cart—used for transporting disabled guests—and re-assembling it in the middle of the Library reference room. Or, smuggling a sheep into the Dean of Students' room on a weekend when the monk was away. As they say around here, when two or three are gathered together, shit happens.

Pranks and laughs aside, Dmitri is serious about who he is and where he's going—and how people see him. As Jane Austen dramatized in her famous novel *Pride and Prejudice*, our first impressions of people can be persuasive and lasting—and totally wrong. Dmitri wants first impressions of him, especially when he's a priest, to be true. "It's a big struggle for guys like me," he said. "I want to get rid of the joking-around manner and be serious, and yet I don't to be so serious that I'm pushing people away. I want a balance."

Dmitri will find that balance, I think. Even if he never becomes a priest, he's grown into the kind of man who is passionate, yet hasn't allowed his passion to control his life. Like Katerina told him, he's someone I'd go to for help or just a listening ear.

Alyosha, who stands at the far end of the railing, is the same height as Dmitri, with roughly the same build. Like Ivan, he is a Senior at Conception Seminary College.

In *The Brothers Karamazov*, the character Alyosha is Dostoevski's "hero"—the one brother most like Dostoevski himself. Religious by instinct rather than will, he is not a fanatic, nor does he judge others; rather, he inspires love.

My Alyosha moves along similar pathways. Soft-spoken, easy-going, and gracious, he has a way of making others feel welcome and appreciated. I have felt that since his first semester at the seminary, when he was one of the young Freshmen in my writing class. Alyosha loves God and he loves people.

He has told me that the possibility of becoming a priest was embedded deep within him since childhood. It isn't surprising. Like Dmitri and Ivan, Alyosha had gone to Catholic schools all his life. His family had strong ties to their urban parish. His father served as both a lector and extraordinary minister of Communion and had considered entering the priesthood when he was young, though he never went to seminary. Alyosha inherited his set of child-sized vestments, made by his grandmother, in which his father used to play "priest." Alyosha's uncle was a priest who had attended Conception in the late 60's and early 70's. Moreover, his mother "adopted" the associate priests of his family's parish, who always felt welcome to drop by their house to relax and turn their cell phones off. From an early age, priests had always been an important part of Alyosha's life.

In high school, Alyosha's priestly ambitions cooled, at least for a time. He was more interested in girls and enjoying life with his friends in Kansas City, where he lived. But in his junior year the call of the priesthood returned.

Having grown up around priests all his life, Alyosha's decision to become a priest himself seemed a natural choice—perhaps too natural. He admits that there was a lot about his faith and the priesthood that he didn't understand because he had always taken it for granted. It was like the air that he breathed. It was perhaps because of this that when Alyosha broached the idea of going to seminary his uncle suggested that he attend a secular college first to taste a different way of life. But Alyosha was stubborn and made the decision to come to Conception Seminary College the year after high school.

Though Conception was familiar ground to him from his Catholic high school retreats here, Alyosha didn't really know what to expect when he arrived as a Freshman seminarian.

Almost at once, he felt overwhelmed. He had been used to a different life as a high school student in Kansas City, with plenty of free time to spend with friends, and a late curfew every night. Now, as a new seminarian, he had to adjust to having almost every hour of his day scheduled. It was discouraging and Alyosha so wanted to leave that he didn't unpack for three months. Then, he said, a Senior he'd come to know and respect told him that he had done the same thing his first semester. It was a turning point for him. He went back to his room, unpacked, and settled in. He's never looked back.

If Dmitri's formation experience was like a clay pot that needed to be broken and re-made, Alyosha's has resembled a steadily maturing plant already rooted in rich earth, a steady deepening and growth of seriousness and certainty in his calling. Still, as he readily admits, every plant must weather storms and frosts, and needs pruning at times. Living in a small, isolated, at times religiously intense community has been a challenge and he's experienced his share of missteps and conflicts. Yet Alyosha has been clear about the benefits of the seminary: It has taught him about life in ways he never would have learned had he not come here. It's taught him a great deal about himself. Though he will probably live alone as a diocesan priest, the give-and-take with his peers has been an essential part of his education.

"I've learned how to deal with people I don't agree with," he said to me recently. "There are always going to be those people who I won't be able to please, especially as a priest. They'll think I'm either too liberal, too conservative, or too middle-of-the-road. In the end, though, those aren't the things that matter the most."

What does matter for Alyosha? Understanding other people, for one. In a seminary, he reflected, the ties of community can be tested by strong religious convictions, by seminarians with differing points of view labeling and judging each other.

"It's okay to have a way of thinking," he said. "To be drawn to a certain style of worship and liturgy, but if you're so rigid that you can't get out of yourself and not understand where someone else is coming from, then you're going to run into big problems down the road."

Since his childhood, Alyosha has been attracted to older forms of liturgy such as the Tridentine Mass, the pre-Vatican II Latin rite. He had some exposure to this rite growing up. Yet he is not romantic about the past. For Alyosha, tradition is something that can inform and enrich the spirituality of the present, provided one understands it and "keeps in thinking with the Church." Conception Seminary College, he says, has helped him to understand this.

It is clear to me that Alyosha, if not a "born priest," will certainly be a gifted one. He has developed a pastoral orientation and consciousness that is able to listen to and love the wide diversity of souls he will encounter in his ministry. What has helped shape this is prayer. That, too, has been a personal journey for him here at the seminary.

Before he came to seminary, Alyosha tended to see his life in compartments, including his religious life: Church was going to mass with his family on Sundays. Even daily mass in high school was simply another part of the day, as reciting the Rosary was part of his night.

Alyosha's formation at Conception Seminary College has drawn these "parts" into an integrated whole. Prayer, rather than being something he does at particular times during the day, now frames and weaves together the different strands of his life. Rather than being something he does, it is more something he *is*. Living and going to school at a Benedictine abbey, being around monks, hearing the bells ringing for prayer each day—these all have had their effect on him. Prayer has sustained him in his life here at Conception; it will continue to sustain him through his years of parish ministry.

My three seminarians—Alyosha, Dmitri, and Ivan—are neither typical nor common. They are individuals out of many who have passed through the doors of this school. Each of them is emerging—at times struggling—out of where he's come from toward where he has chosen to go—toward greater intimacy with God. Whether that life-long pilgrimage will be lived out in the collar and tunic of priest is still an open question for each of them, though not so open as it once was. With each year at the seminary these three seem to be more sure of their call.

The Freshmen awaiting my arrival in the classroom upstairs have only begun this journey. I could tell them what to expect, but they wouldn't listen to what I have to say. The way it is with fathers and sons, I can't make their journey any easier by trying to tell them how it will be. That's the way it has to be, especially here at the seminary. If formation is anything, it's about unveiling the masks of the human heart, that Master Trickster, Tyrant, and Lover, elusive tale-spinner of both deceit and truth.

Chapter Three:
Catholics

※ ※ ※

In the seminary they talk much of formation: academic, character, spiritual. In *Pastores Dabo Vobis*, Pope John Paul II's 1992 apostolic exhortation on the formation of priests, he describes how this process is akin to Jesus' calling of his disciples, asking them "to set aside a period of time for formation."[1] Yet seminary formation does not come out of nothing. The human clay has already been formed by years of elementary and secondary education, whether at an institution like a public or Catholic school, or at home. But the most important formation happens in the family—for better or worse.

When I think of disciples like Peter, Thomas, or Judas Iscariot, I wonder how their early lives shaped them. What did they fear? What did they hope for? Were any of them abused, abandoned, or broken as children? What was religion to them before Jesus called them? Did it give comfort? Truth? A promise of liberation? Or was it a mere motion of the lips, a habit without thought? Or, perhaps, an aching vacancy, until the Son of Man came with his new, disturbing, life-saving words.

My early formation took place on the Mesabi Iron Range of northeast Minnesota, which another Ranger and one of my musical soul-teachers, Bob Dylan, describes as "a little corner of the earth" with "dark frozen woods and icy roads."[2] I remember them well. My father was from Chisholm, made familiar in the movie *Field of Dreams* (though the actual town they used in the film was Galena, Illinois). Archibald "Moonlight" Graham, who played one inning for John McGraw's New York Giants in 1905, was my father's doctor.

Like other Iron Range towns, Chisholm owed its existence to the rich deposits of iron ore in the area. Incorporated as a village in 1901, it grew quickly to a population of over 4,000 by 1905. Its largely immigrant population came from Finland, Austria (Austria-Hungary), Italy, and other parts of Europe. Chisholm, like the other mining towns of the Range, was a rowdy, rough and tumble place, especially in the town's forty-eight saloons. My mom, who is from Ranier, up on the Minnesota-Canadian border, used to hear stories about the Finns down on the Range and the knives that they used when they got into fights.

In the early days on the Range, where your family immigrated from was everything. It was the "race" you belonged to, and you stuck together. Religion tended to harden these ties. In Chisholm, the Italians lived on the south side of town, where the Catholic Church was. My father, a Finn, lived north of Lake Street, the main street that divided Chisholm. The Finns, if they went to church at all, attended the Lutheran church. If a Finn became Catholic through marriage he was considered a traitor to his race. Grudges and grievances could run deep. My father's best friend was Catholic. When he was prohibited from serving as best man at dad's wedding because of his religion, it caused a lasting resentment in my father. Catholicism, for him, came to mean putting religion above friendship.

I was raised in Hoyt Lakes, on the eastern end of the Mesabi Range. The town had been built in the 1950s when taconite mining supplanted the exhausted red-ore mines and new mines like Erie Mining Company, where my father got a job out of college, were shipping taconite pellets by train down to Lake Superior and the ore boats that traversed the Great Lakes to the steel plants in Indiana and Ohio.

Unlike the other Range towns, the houses in Hoyt Lakes were all built at the same time and in nearly the same way, like Abraham Levitt's pre-fabricated community on Long Island. Construction workers put up the houses in a few months as people came from all over the upper Midwest for the new mining jobs. The houses were unpainted—an iron grey siding with steel framed windows that sweated, then froze when the weather got cold. The lawns were dirt and the streets gravel. Later they sodded the lawns, planted trees and paved the streets, giving them English place-names like Hampshire, Suffolk and Canterbury. Eventually, people painted their grey houses, planted gardens, built swing sets and sand boxes, and made something out of a town of nearly identical houses and streets.

Hoyt Lakes was a great place to grow up. It was populated with lots of young families and kids our age. There were stores, churches, playgrounds, ball-fields, a cemetery that was nearly empty; even a beach and a golf course. Steel was in high demand and people made relatively good money in the mines. When they first came to town, people picked out the houses they wanted to live in, and unlike the ethnic and religious "ghettos" of older Range towns, Hoyt Lakes became a heterogeneous mix of Protestant, Catholic, or no particular religion at all. Its gently curving streets gave it the appearance of a suburb that had been detached from a city and dropped into the middle of the north woods.

Had I been conscious of it, I would have seen that my future religious life was being shaped by my family and the historical and social milieu of the Iron Range, especially its politics. As the descendant of immigrant Finns, my father's political heritage was mixed: There were the Church Finns, who came to create a settled, peaceful life, and the Red Finns, who were the leftist agitators and provocateurs. My father was a little of both, though he leaned toward the left in his politics. I can't say that this determined how I turned out politically because my brother, who grew up in the same house, became a conservative Republican.

As for me, there's a little Red Finn in my heart that keeps the fires of revolution stoked; at the same time, the Church Finn is there to throw water on the flames when they get too high. So part of me wants to be a good boy who follows the rules and flosses his teeth every night, while my other side wants to torch the house.

I came of age during the 70's, during the malaise of Watergate and everything afterward. The "credibility gap" and distrust of government is part of my consciousness. I have seen Democrats fail us, and Republicans fail us even worse, while technological development and voracious corporate capitalism have sapped our humanity and laid waste our world. I want a Third Way, something both just and compassionate, thoughtful and tough-minded, responsible and independent. I suspect I want the impossible.

In religion, this adds up to a restless tension of the heart; a deep, anarchic distrust of authorities and hierarchies joined, sometimes uneasily, with an attraction to liturgical order. No wonder I became an Episcopalian. We're small, controversial, liberal some would say, and tenacious about good taste; the religion of former presidents and slave-holders; a liturgical anachronism in a YouTube world. But at our best we welcome to God's table with us the stranger, the sojourner, the doubter and agnostic, the gay and straight, along with the orthodox traditionalist. It's a risky, knife-edge balancing act that keeps getting us into trouble. Still, I wouldn't want to have it any other way.

When I was five years old, some people moved into the house next door to us in Hoyt Lakes. They were the Nelsons and they came from western Minnesota. They were a large family and it wasn't long before the third-oldest boy, David, became my best friend. His father, Helge, was a tall, broad-shouldered, imposing man with a bristling crew-cut. He had accepted a job as principal of Boase Elementary, where my mother taught first grade and where I would soon be attending school. I used to get kidded about having to be a good boy because my mother was a teacher and I lived next door to the principal.

The other thing about the Nelsons is that they were devoutly Catholic. For me, Catholics were a little suspect, an attitude I'd most likely picked up from my father and grandmother. They weren't enemies, but always different. There was something a little strange and cultish about the Catholic kids trooping off to catechism class during the school day at Boase Elementary School. We never really knew where they went, or what they did there, but our schoolwork was suspended while they were absent. It seemed a strange privilege, and though we loved the time we had to mess around, we felt left out of something important. Their church services were special, too, announced by the dramatic sound of a bell ringing from the church spire. My sister remembers wanting to go to mass with the other Catholic girls because they got to wear white gloves and a hats.

The Nelsons were a large family of seven children (that was another thing about Catholics: they seemed to have a lot of children). They were good people. My parents and David's parents became friends, despite my father's lingering resentment of Catholicism. There were tensions in this friendship, though. My father and Helge both had hot tempers. They would start drinking together and soon their voices would rise as they argued about the Vietnam War. Like many Catholics in the 1960's, Helge supported it; my father opposed it.

The Nelson boys loved baseball and they taught me to love it, too. We collected Twins baseball cards with pictures of Harmon Killebrew and Tony Oliva. David's next oldest brother Don was easy-going, with a great sense of humor. Don and his friend Gerald Piper, who lived across the street, usually organized the neighborhood baseball games in an empty field on the edge of town with a diamond made out of rags or pieces of cardboard held down by rocks. I played catch with Don sometimes. Throwing the ball to me, he'd sing the song "Hello Muddah, Hello Faddah," by Allan Sherman.[3]

Don had an infectious laugh and light-hearted personality. I always liked him.

When I was sick I would stay over at the Nelson's house. Don and David's mother took care of me while my mother was teaching first grade at Boase Elementary. Martha Nelson was warm-hearted and devoted to her family, and she cared for me as one of her own. She was a wonderful cook and her baking was extraordinary, especially her chocolate-chip cookies. The night my grandmother died of a heart attack in our house, my brother, sister, and I went to stay at the Nelson's. They were true neighbors to us.

When our family went to church in Hoyt Lakes, it was to the Methodist Church. As far as I can remember, David and I never talked about religion or the differences between us. Yet I remember his First Communion. I remember the Nelson's dinner table set with a white tablecloth and china and how proud his parents were. I had no clue what it was they were celebrating, but it all looked pretty special. Still, I was on the outside looking in. It was different. The Nelsons were normal about other things, but David and his family also belonged to this strange religious world that was a little weird and scary to me. The only time I was ever in the Queen of Peace Catholic Church was when my grandmother took me there for bingo night. She didn't like Catholics, but she liked playing bingo.

Then the Nelsons moved away and I started riding the bus to high school in Aurora, a town five miles west of Hoyt Lakes. There I met a lot of new kids my age, some of them Catholic, some of them girls. The Catholic girls I dated—or wanted to date—had a mysterious and unapproachable attraction about them. Like the Mother Church itself looks to me here in my later life. Back then, religion didn't matter much to me. Not until my conversion at the end of eleventh grade.

After that, my new-found Evangelicalism convinced me that Catholic kids weren't serious about their faith. They drank and smoked. They worshiped Mary rather than Jesus. They didn't really know Jesus as their Lord and Savior like I did. They got baptized when they were infants and were considered "in," no matter what they did after that. If a member of the family decided to become a priest, they believed the whole family had special favor from God, like getting free tickets to the World Series because your son is one of the umpires. So I thought.

This attitude in me changed, but it took years. I think it was actually getting to know Catholics who were serious about their faith. I knew them in college, in graduate school, in life. My brother, who had never taken to Evangelicalism the way I had and was always drawn toward a more liturgical form of worship, became a Catholic. I was at his reception into the Church at the Easter Vigil at St. Mary's Basilica in Minneapolis.

I was glad that Kurt had found a faith he could feel at home in. My father had passed away by the time Kurt converted and I can't help but wonder what he would have thought about it. I can't be sure any more. Dad converted to Christianity while watching Oral Roberts on television, a few months before he died of a brain aneurism. The circumstance of his conversion was one of God's more unexpected ironies: Dad was never comfortable with salesmen, whether of religion, cars, or religion, cars, or anything else.

Coming to Conception Abbey for me was an even deeper plunge into the mysteries of Catholicism. By then I'd been an Episcopalian a few years. My wife and I, burned-out refugees from Evangelicalism, had been wandering in the wilderness for several years. We had checked out several churches in Madison, settling for awhile with the Dutch at a campus Reformed church, Geneva Chapel. There, a deeply thoughtful minister named Andy DeJong helped us find a home for a time. But it didn't last. Not until Pentecost, 1988, when we tasted the sumptuous, sensual feast of high Anglican worship at Grace Episcopal Church in Madison did we feel like we'd come home. Accepting the job at Conception didn't seem like such a large spiritual leap from there.

Before we left Madison for good I ran into an acquaintance from the reformed church we had attended several years before and when he asked me about the job and I told him where I was going he said in a rather ominous tone: "and you don't have a problem with that?" A problem with working for Catholics? No, I told him. I didn't. I was feeling pretty self-satisfied at the time. I'd found a job. What else did I have to worry about?

If I had only been dabbling my feet in Catholic culture before, coming to work at Conception Abbey was like being dropped into the deep end of the pool, or (some days) on an alien planet. I was a Protestant lefty fresh from graduate school in Madison, the "third coast," though the city had been gentrified since the bomb-throwing days of the late 1960s. Now I found myself at a Catholic seminary in rural Missouri.

I get surprised by this sometimes and the kind of tensions it can foster. A couple of years ago one of my former students, who had often acted as a political ideologue in class, returned for a brief visit to the seminary. He saw me on the sidewalk and blurted out, "are you still here?" Even after seventeen years of teaching at Conception I still found myself coiling for a defensive strike. *Why wouldn't I be?* The thought flared in my brain, even as he was smiling and extending his hand toward me in greeting. But his remark grated on me for days and I wondered if it was because I had so often asked the same question myself.

For most of my years at the seminary, I have taught students who came of age within the impressively long reign of John Paul II. His approach to strong moral conviction, to solid Catholic doctrine, and to social justice has shaped their outlook as Catholics. They are serious about their faith. They wouldn't be here otherwise. They've come to Conception Abbey because someone—usually a priest—asked them a simple but potentially life-changing question: "Have you ever thought about the priesthood?" Some have. Some, indeed, like Ivan and Alyosha, have thought about it since they were young, serving as altar boys or being strongly influenced by a parent or grandparent, uncle or brother-in-law. I've had students who knew little about the priesthood or even what a seminary was before they came here. Someone popped the question and they came. Becoming a priest is a tough choice in a society that in recent years has looked on the Catholic priesthood with suspicion. I admire them for their courage and commitment.

Einstein said, "A foolish faith in authority is the worst enemy of truth." What is the measure of foolishness, and are there authorities we can put our faith in? That's the Protestant question. If not the pope, if not the magisterium, if not the force of history and tradition, what? Can the inner voice, the individual discernment of truth, be enough? Though I am Protestant, I can no longer answer this question with any certainty. What I do know is that the distinction Jesus makes is not between "conservative" and "liberal," "orthodox" and "unorthodox," but between those who love their neighbor and those who don't. Who is our neighbor? That person next to us. The lost. The grief-stricken. The homeless. The hungry. The outcast. The stranger.

Ivan, Dmitri and Alyosha stand above me as I climb the stairs. I am their teacher, their master, and their servant—and they are mine as well. These are stand-up guys. Like our neighbors, the Nelsons, they will pray for me and my family, worry about me, ask me how I'm doing. In short, they care for me in the way God cares for me. I never realized how important that was until last winter when I was lying in a hospital bed waiting for the results of an MRI scan that I hoped would tell me why I was experiencing nervous system disorders. I expected the worst and fear screamed bloody death in my brain. Then I was reminded of these seminarians and their prayers. Somehow, I found peace.

As I reach the top of the stairs, Ivan nods his head at me and smiles, as does Alyosha. Dmitri lifts his hand in greeting, a roguish half-smile on his face. "Morning, Doc," he says. That's how he normally addressed me. Or he'll call me "Dr. J." I spend a minute or so talking to him, as more students and monks enter through the front doors below. The day has begun.

Chapter Four:
Telling Stories

❖ ❖ ❖

By the time I reach the classroom, they've been here for almost ten minutes, talking, staring at nothing in particular, or resting their heads on the tables in front of them. Like Ivan, Dmitri, and Alyosha, they've just come from Morning Prayer, flowing down from the Holy Cross Oratory on the fourth floor of St. Maur Hall like a heavy, somnolent fog. It can be a challenging daily discipline for them, characterized by one of the seminarians in a pungent haiku:
Morning Prayer; early
Attendance mandatory
Damn sockless fetor[1]

The lights in the classroom room are still turned off and, with the blinds closed, its half-dark in the room. I flip on the light switch. The ones who don't have their heads down on the tables recoil, shrieking in mock horror, like vampires caught by the dawn.

There are twenty-four Freshmen in Writing I this semester. That's a sizeable class for this seminary, whose total student population is less than a hundred. It's diverse, too. They come from a lot of different places in the United States, between the Rockies and the Appalachians, and beyond: Mexico, Venezuela, Bolivia, Kenya, Vietnam. A quarter of the students sitting before me aren't native to this country.

They're young and, despite appearances at eight-thirty in the morning, eager to please. They want to be pure; they want to be worthy; they want to get good grades. There's a raw, unformed, unjaded quality about them that on most days I love. This morning, it's good to see all of them.

This course—Writing I—is normally about writing but today I'm going to read them a story. They're beginning work on their first full essay of the semester, a narrative, and I want to show them how to write prose that grabs the reader and doesn't let go. There are other, riskier things I want them to get from the class today, but that's the main goal. The story I've chosen is "How to Tell a True War Story," by Tim O'Brien, from *The Things They Carried*.[2]

I like teaching O'Brien because his stories are easy to read, yet challenging to understand. I use them as a kind of pedagogical Trojan Horse to penetrate the sometimes obstinate walls of my students' resistance to books. Moreover, the stories are about war, a subject my young male students get into—those who have not known it firsthand. Yet war is the vehicle for other things O'Brien wants to say. Like Hemingway's fiction, there's a lot going on under the surface of a Tim O'Brien story.

O'Brien shares a trait with other writers I teach here like Homer, Shakespeare, Hawthorne, Dostoevsky, Remarque,

Kafka, Hemingway, Joyce, Hurston, Ellison, O'Connor, Nabokov, Percy, Welty, Wiesel, Atwood. Like them, he doesn't give answers, but instead re-creates the questions that can't be answered, only re-told. My questions.

I start reading the story aloud to them. As I do, I can see that most are falling in with me, but a few lag behind. They are somewhere other than here, in this classroom: their dorm room, the open road, even all the way back home, wondering why they have been sent by their bishops to this place in the middle of the middle of nowhere. They've only been here for a couple of weeks and it's too early yet for the pain of homesickness to have passed out of their eyes and the hunch of their bodies in the chairs. They look cold.

Of course, I may be wrong about this. It's early in the morning and the glazed, hammered look in their eyes may simply be the lingering stains of sleep. This is the challenge: to take them from where they are and bring them *inside*, where learning happens. I'm hoping O'Brien will help me with that today, but like teaching anything, it's always only a hope.

This morning, however, the story works: Word by word, sentence by sentence, O'Brien's story takes my students out of northwest Missouri and into Vietnam, four decades ago. We're with Alpha Company: Lieutenant Jimmy Cross, Rat Kiley, Stink Harris, Mitchell Sanders, Norman Bowker, Kiowa, and Curt Lemon, who's going to die. We move with them across the river toward the mountains. The land is silent and strange, and it's dark like twilight under the giant trees.

It's more than a little unreal, too, for them as well as me. I was in elementary school when the Vietnam War started and in high school when it ended. I experienced the war by way of television, through Walter Cronkite's nightly tally of the killed and wounded, through the lens of the cameramen and the words of correspondents. I didn't know anyone in my hometown who had actually gone to the war. I was just a kid growing up in northeast Minnesota and didn't understand the war or even care. I didn't know the jungle.

Yet there are some here in my class today who do. Alfredo is one. He sits to my left, near the end of one of the rows of desks. He's one of half a dozen students here from Latin America. Solidly built with dark eyes, a crew cut, and a winning smile, he listens intently to O'Brien's story. Because it's not his native language, listening to English read aloud is easier for him than reading it.

Alfredo hates war, but he listens—and the memories come. He has told me about them: Back in the 1980's, when he was a young boy living in El Salvador the guerrilla soldiers came to his house one night and his family fled into the jungle. There they waited, his mother's hand pressed over Alfredo's mouth so he would make no noise to give them away. That night the soldiers murdered his uncle, who lived in the house next door.

When Alfredo turned sixteen, his parents sent him out of the country to avoid compulsory military service. He traveled along a dangerous route through Guatemala and Mexico north toward the United States, escorted by the *coyotes*, the ruthless men who traffic in human beings. Alfredo is at the seminary because he wants to do something good with his life. He wants to be a priest.

In the story we've come to the trail junction, where Mitchell Sanders spins his yo-yo while Rat Kiley and Curt Lemon play around with a smoke grenade, tossing it back and forth between them. Then Lemon steps on a booby trap: a rigged 105 round. His sudden death is described four separate times in the story as a kind of gruesome transfiguration. Each version is more detailed, more emotionally intense than the last. It's as if the narrator were working out something in therapy, trying to uncover a long-suppressed trauma.

The students are all with me now, listening intently as O'Brien does one of his post-modern twists, bringing the narrator right out of the story to talk to us, like a director interrupting his own movie to comment on the action. He talks about what's true and what's false and how hard it is to actually keep those things straight sometimes in a war story, or in any story: Things get missed, or remembered wrongly, or exaggerated—or even made up. Yet, somehow, it's still true. That's the paradox of stories.

The story ends. I wait a few moments. It's quiet in the classroom and I wonder what these guys are thinking, feeling. Are they moved at all by what they've heard? Or have all the images of death flowing across their televisions and computer screens numbed them to the effects of a story like O'Brien's?

Tentatively, as if waking someone from sleep, I begin asking them questions.

O'Brien's narrator claims that a true war story is "never about war." I ask them what this means. I can see some small frowns, a half-grin or two, or a slight glaze over some of their eyes. They know I want something but they can't figure out what it is. Most of them don't look at me, afraid I'll call on them if we make eye contact. It's the usual classroom game. After more silence, I repeat the question.

"If this story isn't about war, what's it about?"

"Telling stories," one of my students dead-pans, then gives me a small, ironic smile. He's one of the brighter bulbs in the class and I can't help thinking he can see right through me—all my tricks, my disguises.

I feel the let-down of the paint-by-number, fill-in-the-blank quality of this discussion, which is not a discussion really but an exercise in getting them to give me the right answer. It's a set-up, in other words: We teachers want our students to think for themselves and we also want them to think like us. Paradox or folly, this is what teachers usually want, even though we might delude ourselves into thinking that we don't.

So I decide to push things farther; O'Brien's story has brought us there anyway.

"What's he saying about truth?"

They look at me, unsure of what to say, so no one says anything. Who wants to look stupid? Besides, they probably suspect that I'm leading them into strange, ambiguous territory where things are not always what they seem.

With some exceptions, my seminarians are challenged by the kinds of ambiguity found in literature. They want a more straightforward pathway to the truth. Yet I have seen some of them take the road of learning that is less traveled as they have opened themselves to the subtle mystery of stories.

"Are the stories here true?" I ask.

"Sort of," someone says. A pretty good answer. We talk about the character Rat Kiley, whose stories are always exaggerated, and sometimes even total fabrications. Yet they are also true. Surprisingly, some of my students seem to like this idea. I tell them it's not relativism or moral anarchy, but simply the currency of the human condition—and the stuff of stories, whether they're reading O'Brien or the Old Testament. I'm not sure they believe me.

For many of them, learning how to think about things like this—about how stories work—is not what they think they need from a seminary education. My students want to learn stuff, but like other college students at most colleges and universities in the United States, they're pragmatic: they want what they think they're going to use, or what they have to know for the test. They want me to give them answers. I try to give them something else.

I ask them more questions about O'Brien. The discussion gets some speed, and even leaves the ground for awhile. That's the best I can hope for at this time of the morning, but it's still a bit of a let-down. As a teacher, I want more. I always do.

The class ends and something unexpected happens: While most of the students head for the door, a few of them approach me as I'm gathering up my notes at the podium in front of class. There's genuine excitement in their eyes: "I want to write my story like O'Brien's," one of them says to me. "How do I do that?"

It's a tough question to answer in the few minutes we have, so I set up some appointments for office hours and leave the classroom feeling like I've moved the markers ahead a little: Small successes, small victories, a mind or two or three opened another fraction, a question planted, like a mustard seed.

There are times when I feel like a drudge, working an assembly line in a small education factory, installing the necessary parts. At those times I lose my faith in teaching, in books and writing. Then I see my students drawn into the heart of a story like Tim O'Brien's and I become a believer again in what I do here at the seminary—that it matters for the future lives of my students.

Father Scott Boeckman, a priest in Oklahoma and former student of mine, told me that one of his most significant moments of learning at Conception Seminary College came when he read *The Plague*, by Albert Camus, in one of my courses.

That novel, which tells of an epidemic of bubonic plague in the North African city of Oran during the 1940's, is a kind of extended, dramatized debate between people with radically different philosophies of life, all under the absurd condemnation of the plague. Some are Christian, some atheist, some stoic, some cowards, survivors, or opportunists. It's a grim story: As the townspeople die in horrible pain and hope wanes, the question of the meaning of innocent suffering and death is made excruciatingly clear. Camus gives no answer to that question, only a story. But what a story. Fr. Scott says it helped prepare him for what he would face as a priest.

His whole life Fr. Scott has been a pilgrim, a seeker, asking big questions about himself and the world: Why are we here? What is the purpose of life? As he has told me, in his experience of the world beyond seminary and theology school—the world of the American Catholic parish—easy answers don't work very well. But then answers are not what a priest is called to give to people—to the pregnant teenager, the man dying of AIDS, the bankrupt farmer. Rather, the priest is called to give himself, a broken, imperfect human being, and what power he has comes through his own wounded powerlessness and faith.

I remember something Fr. Andrew Greeley said about why he's a Catholic, that it has a lot to do with the stories and images of his faith, of the Eucharist and the Madonna.[3] Though I am not Catholic, my faith, like the faith of my students, or the faith of the monks, comes ultimately from storytelling, from God himself, who told us about the Kingdom in stories.

In the beginning is the Story. A tissue of lies–and the truth I live by. Through books, I teach the tenacious uncertainties, and stubborn hope, of my own life and faith.

Chapter Five: Communion

❖ ❖ ❖

September nears its end. The steady rhythm of teaching, class preparation and my other duties here at the seminary has quickened the pace of the days and weeks. I am reminded of the passing of time by the ripening of the soybeans in the fields that has cast a rich ochre coverlet over the lingering green of summer.

For the Roman Catholic Church, as well as the so-called mainline Protestant churches, time is measured by a different rhythm, yet one that is linked to the passing of the natural seasons: Advent, with its wintry introspection leading into the rich abundance of Christmas, followed by Epiphany and then Lent, which in northern climates coincides with the long, dark wait for spring; then comes the glorious vernal resurrection of Easter and the steady growth into the green of ordinary time, beyond Pentecost.

In my youth I was completely ignorant of the seasons of the church year. I used to think that the twelve days of Christmas were a kind of countdown to the moment when I could open presents on Christmas Eve. After all, that interminable song, "The Twelve Days of Christmas," sung by Dinah Shore on a Christmas album we had at home, was all about receiving gifts.

Evangelical conversion didn't enlighten me much about the church year: Christmas and Easter were celebrated with special intensity, but we had no Advent, Epiphany, or Lent. No stained glass or candles. No images. No liturgy other than the ad hoc kind that most evangelical churches adopt as a prelude to the main event of the service, the sermon. No saints. Nothing that might diffuse or corrupt a direct, personal, unmediated contact with God. I didn't know what I was missing.

Today is the Feast of St. Wenceslaus. This isn't a fact I normally carry around in my head. I learned it from Fr. Donald Grabner this morning. Sometimes Fr. Donald will greet me in the faculty lounge with a good morning and an acknowledgment of the feast day, if it's at all significant. Some days I'll ask him. Today was one of those days: Wenceslaus isn't a major feast in anyone's calendar, except in Bohemia.

Though the veneration of saints has been a central part of Catholic spirituality for centuries, to most Protestants they occupy an alien, suspect religious territory: Saints seem to belong to that apocryphal, hocus-pocus aspect of religion that has nothing to do with salvation.

Joining the Episcopal Church immersed me in liturgy and the redemptive rhythm of the church year. It felt like coming home to a sense of sanctified time that appealed to my sacramental imagination. Still, saints have only slowly become a part of my spiritual consciousness, and that only through being here at the seminary. They help me to remember God's care for his people through the eternal body of believers—dead, living, and yet to come. But I can't pray to them. Not yet, anyway.

As for Wenceslaus—"Good King Wenceslaus," as the ancient song describes him—he was a Christian king in the tenth century and patron saint of Bohemia, where my mother's family originated. Among saints he represents a rare ideal in the world: the pursuit of the good in political life. This is not a likely prospect at any time, even with born-again presidents. Like anyone who attempts reform, Wenceslaus made enemies. The good king was assassinated on his way to mass one day.

The monks usually take their monastic names from saints. If I were to ever become a monk I would ask my abbot to name me after St. Joseph. He is here in front of me, on the steps before the building that bears his name. I look up at his face, cut in white marble. It is partly turned toward the boy Jesus in his arms, whose tiny hands are spread wide in blessing. Joseph is depicted as a young man, bearded, and his eyes show a calm, focused tenderness echoed in his son's expression. From the top of his staff there blooms a flower. Together, these two figures express the loving compassion of God for a broken world.

I am drawn to Joseph mostly because he was a father—Jesus' foster-father, according to tradition. As my own son nears the time when he will leave home for college, I think of Joseph losing his own son. We know of Mary's sorrow at the foot of the cross, but what of Joseph? Had he died by then, as some of the traditions say? Was he spared such tragic knowledge, leaving Mary to bear it alone? Did Joseph suspect, perhaps, that his son would die?

Jesus loved because he was loved. I know that much. The family who raises us also teaches us to love, or not to love.

God the Father gave Jesus to parents who loved him, I believe, and so did he learn to love others. And with love comes the tragedy of love: that one must endure the loss of the loved one. Fathers and mothers love their children and then lose them to the inevitable cycle of life as they grow to adulthood and leave home to begin creating their own lives. Sometimes they lose them too early: to death, as Mary lost Jesus.

These thoughts—somber on such a bright, beautiful morning—are interrupted by the sound of bells. From the basilica tower above they ring out for mass, which will begin in a few minutes. I turn away from the statue of Joseph and Jesus, glancing northeast where the fields roll on in green folds toward a distant tower rising above the trees. It is the monastery at Clyde, where the Benedictine Sisters of Perpetual Adoration live. If possible, Clyde is more remote than Conception. Driving out there feels a little like falling off the edge of the world, and finding a bed of peace.

Students hurry toward me across the courtyard from their rooms in St. Michael Hall. Dmitri is one of them. He slows to walk with me along the colonnade of St. Joseph Hall and we talk a little.

I'm going to mass today not because of St. Wenceslas or St. Joseph, but because I want to. I don't have to attend—it's not an obligation, even for Catholic faculty and staff. The students are required to attend; I am subject only to my ecumenical whims.

Following Dmitri into the basilica, I see him dip his fingers into the marble font just inside the door and make the sign of the cross across his chest. I look at the water of the font, its surface disturbed by ripples running across its clear surface.

With a slight hesitation, I wet the tips of my fingers and, like Dmitri, make the sign of the cross.

This is a slightly uncomfortable act for me here in the Catholic house of worship. I do it because I want to and, I must admit, because I can. Who would stop me? Besides, I like doing it: It's a physical sign of my baptism as well as my devotion to God. After years of living within an evangelical religious culture that rejects most physical signs as pagan idolatry, I came to realize how impoverished my spiritual life had been.

At the same time I feel somewhat self-conscious, as if I were playing make-believe with Catholic devotional piety, and I can't help thinking that everyone is looking at me. There are also my inner voices of skepticism toward religious pieties. Shall I act for me, or for the voices in my head? It's the classic existential moment, straight out of Jean-Paul Sartre: what is the authentic thing to do?

Well, this is too much head-noise for me right now. I find a place to sit down ten pews back on the left-hand side of the nave. I'm sitting in the middle of the area where the seminarians usually sit. A few nod at me as I come in. Most are reluctant to sit in the same pew as me, like it's a zone of intimidation. I am the Professor, after all.

As I sit and wait for the mass to begin, my eyes find their way forward, upward, as they always do here in the basilica. The space is designed to transport the sight and spirit toward the altar and beyond, to the magnificent image of Mary Immaculate, the Blessed Mother enthroned amid the stars of heaven on the curved ceiling of the apse at the far end of the nave. The play of light from the high windows and the plain, subdued colors, as well as the Romanesque simplicity of the architectural design, calms the mind. As one of my students said, "it's easy to pray in here." I have to agree with him.

The basilica was dedicated on May 10, 1891, almost twenty years after Frowin Conrad and the monks from Engelberg Abbey first arrived at Conception to found a monastery. Unfortunately, a tornado largely severely damaged the church two years later. When it was rebuilt, Beuronese murals of the lives of Mary and St. Benedict and St. Scholastica were added. The church was designated a minor basilica by Pope Pius XII in 1941, the first one west of the Mississippi. The latest renovation was completed in 1999.

I remember the way it looked in here before the renovation. The interior was dark, with a traditional design inconvenient for the liturgical reforms of the 1960s. Still, for all its limitations, I loved it and the sense I always had of its age and historical significance—young by European standards yet, but a singular architectural monument out here on this windy ridge in northwest Missouri.

Dmitri has taken his place in a pew in front of me with a couple of his friends. Ivan is seated further forward; Alyosha, somewhere behind me. People are still coming into the church; Monks and students, people from the community. As the seminarians enter from St. Joseph Hall and walk back along the north aisle, they pause and turn to face the Blessed Sacrament Chapel, directly across the nave. Here, they genuflect, sinking to one knee before the Tabernacle, which is contained in a tabernacle in the chapel.

Yet in the people who kneel I recognize genuine devotion, an acknowledgment of the presence of Christ in that small octagonal room across the nave. My mind starts wandering away, out from under this vast star-gilt ceiling toward the mysterious corridors and closed anterooms of Catholic Things: Mary, the Rosary, the Blessed Sacrament, the Real Presence, Transubstantiation.

Not long ago, a Catholic friend of mine asked me if I had ever considered becoming Catholic. It was a delicate question, asked with consummate grace and tender reluctance. I would have probably dismissed it, had it come from anyone else. I understood, too, that it was a question of whether I *would* become Catholic, a question, in other words, of spiritual discernment.

Now this question returns, hijacking my attention, abducting me into the closet of *reasons*. Watching the seminarians genuflecting, I glance toward the Blessed Sacrament Chapel and wonder: could I do this? For the cradle Catholic it seems straightforward; but for this Protestant, it isn't so simple. For the cradle Catholic it seems straightforward, there is no need to think about *being* Catholic—one simply *is*. It is a habit of the body and heart, even for those who lapse or leave. But a convert, especially one who has moved from strong affinity with another faith, has a more difficult path, requiring serious intellectual assent.

Monks are entering the basilica from the monastery, finding their places in the choir. A few visitors seat themselves on the other side of the nave. Mass begins. Word, prayer and song rise toward the arch-framed vaults of the high ceiling. I am at home with the shape of this worship, close as it is to that of the Episcopal Church. More importantly, I am drawn into a sense of being part of a community—until we reach the Rite of the Eucharist.

For me, this is the hard part. Communion here, as elsewhere within Roman Catholicism, is for Catholics only.

This is why I normally don't attend mass at Conception except on special occasions or when I am required to attend, such as the Graduation Mass at the end of the school year. I am here today because I am feeling the need for being with the monks and students in worship. At this moment, however, I can't help but feel cut off from them, as if I were attending a banquet, watching the others eat as I sit before an empty plate.

When I was an evangelical, none of this would have mattered to me. That changed as Carolyn and I found our way to the Anglican liturgy and sacrament of the Episcopal Church. The Eucharist became an altar call we could both live with. We're still not sure what it's all about, exactly: Bread and wine and something more, because it's from God. Presence, certainly. Love, undoubtedly. I guess we're typically Anglican in our uncertainties. The best I can say is that the Eucharist, like baptism, is a mystery: a sacramental, symbolic poetry that can't be explained. What Carolyn and I are sure about is how much communion matters to us.

The seminarians are naturally curious about what Episcopalians believe. They've heard things about us, of course: we're the ones with women priests and (openly) gay bishops. We reside in a messy, sometimes muddled, middle ground—the *Via Media*—between tradition and innovation. Liturgically, our faith is more Catholic than Protestant. It is certainly far different from the Protestantism of my young adulthood.

I have at various times described to seminarians a typical service in an evangelical church. It is centered on the sermon, I tell them. Communion only occurs, at the most, once each month, depending upon the particular congregation. In the Swedish Baptist church where my wife was raised, it consisted of a small cup of grape juice and a small cube of white bread passed to everyone in the pews. In Carolyn's memory, communion always felt like an add-on to the real purpose of church: answering the question of eternal salvation.

When I tell them this, those seminarians who are not converts from Protestantism will look at me with brows furrowed in disbelief: *How can people believe that this is Christianity?* I can practically hear the question banging around in their skulls. Then I speak their thought aloud, adding: "Of course, they think the same about you. In fact, many don't think you're Christians." I usually get an incredulous laugh from them when I say this.

As the seminarians around me stand and move toward the aisle, I move with them. Though I will not receive communion, I seek to be part of this mass, this community, and ask for a blessing from the celebrant. We advance in two lines up the aisle to where Fr. Albert Bruecken stands distributing wafers. Ahead of me I see some seminarians receiving the wafer in their open hands; some directly on their tongues. Some walk directly up to Fr. Albert to receive it; others genuflect first.

I reach the head of the line. I am conscious of a desire to take the wafer from Fr. Albert, but it won't do. Instead, I step forward and fold my arms over my chest to refuse the communion wafer. I ask Fr. Albert for a blessing and he places his hand lightly on my forehead. His fingers are warm and so are his words. In them I feel once again the bonds of friendship and love that have embraced me, once a stranger from a far country, here at Conception Abbey. Then I turn away.

Monks and students will tell me how glad they are to see me when I do show up to mass, and I appreciate that. Still, this moment makes me sad and I experience again the tragedy of the Reformation. If I were only a day-tripper here it would be different. Because of my relationship with the monks and students, the exclusion brings with it pain. Yet this pain is knowledge, too, and a sharpening of vision for what binds us together, and what transforms us.

Occasionally here at the seminary I have taught the work of a Danish philosopher named Søren Kierkegaard, who is sometimes called the Father of Existentialism. He's also the father of some particularly unreadable sentences, such as this one: "The self is a relation that relates itself to itself or is the relation's relating itself to itself in the relation; the self is not the relation but is the relation's relating itself to itself."[1] The titles of his books can be off-putting, too: *The Concept of Anxiety*, *Fear and Trembling*, and *The Sickness Unto Death*. You just have a feeling that reading any of these isn't going to be much fun.

As a college student I tried reading Kierkegaard because a teacher I respected told me "S.K.," as he called the philosopher, was important. I tried—and quickly gave up. I was young and impatient and Kierkegaard was too oblique for me. A few years later I tried again. And again. Kierkegaard finally took hold of me when I discovered "Diary of a Seducer" in *Either/Or*. Then I tackled the *Concluding Unscientific Postscript*, another page-turning title, but the most important of his books. To my surprise, it was interesting—even engrossing—because it dealt with the question of what it means to be a Christian.

I've found ways to bring the Danish Lutheran Kierkegaard into the seminary because I believe that what he has to say is important for Catholic seminarians to hear. To put it simply, Kierkegaard's writing is concerned with the question of authentic faith and the conversion of the individual.

Whether we are Protestant or Catholic, conversion matters. Evangelicals know this well. I have discovered that Catholics know it, too. Father Xavier Nacke, the spiritual director for the seminary, has talked about the importance of conversion within the lives of the seminarians: "It's crucial that they see this," he said to me one day. I thought it was interesting, this talk of conversion, coming from a Catholic priest and monk. But that's really what spiritual formation is all about: We surrender what we have and what we are to God; he breaks and blesses it, then gives it back to us transformed.

There's a novel by James Joyce entitled *A Portrait of the Artist as a Young Man* that I occasionally teach here at Conception, not only because of its literary merit, but because its about a young man discerning his call to the priesthood. *Portrait* is a spiritual text, despite the fact that Joyce had abandoned his faith at the time he wrote it and made Stephen Dedalus, his protagonist, abandon it, too, for the life of the artist. It was this book that led Thomas Merton into the Catholic Church. The novel appeals to seminarians because Stephen is like them: a young man discerning a call to a priestly vocation. They relate to his anguish and confusion and, for a few of them, his religious doubt.

I used to imagine the journey of faith as a sudden flash from the sky followed by a steady progress of spiritual enlightenment. But what the seminarians of Conception have taught me is that the road of conversion and discernment can be long, confusing, painful, messy journey, with an uncertain outcome. In other words, it is a very human journey through many detours and false turns, sort of like driving down a road at night: sometimes you can't see any farther than what's in the headlights, and sometimes you can't even see that far.

I know this road. I once went through a discernment process for the priesthood within the Episcopal Church, before faith took flight. During that time, which lasted about a year, I applied myself to piety. I was going to be a priest. I was going to be different, because I believed that God had called me to be that way.

So I tried to be different. It took me farther and farther away from my family and from who I was, an ordinary guy stumbling through life, trying to fathom a world that seemed to accelerate and grow more absurd with each passing year.

The call turned out to be a wrong number—or so I thought at the time. I believe now that I was being called, but to something more fundamental. I'm still not sure what that is beyond my ordinary day to day existence teaching at a small Catholic seminary here in the northwest corner of Missouri. The call is to be here for the seminarians and to be among them, to teach them not only how to write and read and think, but also to show them how a person of another faith lives that faith out, however imperfectly. To teach them to love learning, and not to be afraid of knowledge. And to learn. More than anything else, I am called here to learn.

Mass has concluded and I walk out of the basilica with Ivan, Dmitri, and Alyosha. We have sat, stood, kneeled, sung and prayed together. Now we're on our way to the refectory for lunch, where we'll share a feast together. In these three seminarians I will glimpse those things I keep giving to God to be broken and blessed—and transformed: in Ivan, my need to be in control of my life; in Dmitri, my passion and rebellion; and in Alyosha, my need to love and be loved.

Chapter Six:
Brothers in Black

✣ ✣ ✣

September has gone and October is passing, with bright, cool days and longer, colder nights. This morning I'm walking in the St. Columba Cemetery, which lies just across the county road that runs north of the Abbey basilica. Townspeople from Conception and the surrounding countryside are buried here. Monks are buried here, too.

I like this place. I like to walk here when I need to clear my head. Except for occasional cars that pass by on the road, it's peaceful here today under a pale blue sky lightly brushed with white cirrus clouds. The sunlight has the subdued, tawny quality of high autumn, throwing everything into luminous clarity. The brilliantly colored maple leaves above me seem to capture the light like photoelectric cells, giving it back with a strange intensity.

Since today is Thursday, I'll be teaching Existentialism later this morning. It's a hybrid philosophy and literature course that I have offered in the seminary every couple of years. We're nearly finished with the philosophical part of the course and have read works by Kierkegaard, Nietzsche, and Heidegger. Today, we're beginning our month-long dance with the philosophy and fiction of Jean-Paul Sartre.

"Hell is—other people," Sartre famously wrote in his play, *No Exit*.[1] There are days when I can't help agreeing with him. Other people do get in my way, with their expectations and demands for my time and attention. Meanwhile, the voice of the world shouts at me daily to gorge my soul with commodities and ideology, feeding my fear of not getting enough of whatever it is I think I need. Welcome to Hell.

It's tempting to imagine that a place like Conception Abbey, with its isolated, bucolic peace, is an escape from all that: a heaven rather than a hell. The monks would tell you a different story. A Benedictine monastery is not an escape from other people. It's no panacea, but a day-to-day reality of community with all of its pitfalls and opportunities, a workshop of the human soul where, like any workshop, things can get messy.

Novice Andrew Sheller made the decision to enter the monastery during his senior year in the seminary. He was in my existentialism course that fall. At the close of the final class, he asked me about directing an independent study in existential philosophy the following semester. The course had meant a great deal to him personally and he wanted more. I don't credit this to my teaching but, rather, to the very relevant, humanistic focus of the existentialists: They deal with life as it is lived in the world.

I had no clue that Andy's enthusiasm for existential philosophy was rooted in something deeper. He had come to the seminary intent on the priesthood, but found himself being drawn to a life of prayer within a community such as Conception. Then he read Sartre in my course, and, like many other seminarians before him, was inspired by the French philosopher's emphasis on freedom, responsibility, and living the authentic life. It pushed him to make a decision. As he told me later, "I knew that if I wanted a better prayer life, I couldn't just talk about it."

Andy made the leap, and to me it's a pleasing irony that the philosophy of Sartre, the celebrated atheist, became a catalyst for a young man to enter the monastic life.

It's a life few in our society would choose to live. There's no money in becoming a monk, no fame, very little power. To the outsider it seems like it's just a bunch of celibate guys praying and working together in what is essentially a big brick dormitory out in the middle of the Missouri cornfields. The whole thing is so out of sync with the main rhythms of American life that it seems a wonder anyone would seriously *want* to join a monastery.

St. Benedict, the founder of the Benedictine order, designed it that way. He advised that the would-be monk be kept waiting outside the monastery for four or five days to test the seriousness of his intentions.[2] Nowadays it's easier to enter a monastery like Conception, though it's not so easy to stay, especially with everything else in the world there is to do and to be.

For persons entering a community like this one, whether they are lay employees like me, or would-be monks, expectations can run up against some hard realities. What comes afterward depends upon the person: A time of disillusionment and, given enough time and patience, discovery and growth—or frustration. Some make it; many don't, and not because they're selfish or weak. The monastery, after all, is like a family business, with a family's spoken and unspoken rules and expectations.

A young man might choose to enter the monastic life because he wants to be closer to God. Or he wants something else, like escape or therapy. Whatever the motivation, he becomes a novice. His novitiate lasts a year and a day, during which he learns the Rule of St. Benedict, taught to him by the Novice Master.

The Rule, as the monks refer to it, was composed by St. Benedict of Nursia sometime in the early sixth century. By this time the Roman Empire had fallen and the Italian peninsula was in political chaos. Desiring to live a life of religious devotion, St. Benedict left Rome and went to Subiaco, in the Sabine Hills. There he lived in a cave and learned ascetical practices. Two years later he founded a monastery on Monte Cassino. This was the beginning of the Benedictine order.

The Rule St. Benedict created is based on earlier guides to monastic life. It's a combination of practical management guide and wisdom book, mapping out a pathway for living well. Though to modern eyes its instructions sound stringent and even harsh, it is tempered by St. Benedict's voice of fatherly love: "Listen carefully, my son, to the master's instructions, and attend to them with the ear of your heart," he writes at the opening of the Rule. "This is advice from a father who loves you; welcome it, and faithfully put it into practice."[3]

The Rule establishes practical guidelines for a life of stability, fidelity, and self-discipline. For this reason, it continues to be a rich source for living the spiritual life, even amid the frenetic pace and engorged materialism of our affluent, media-saturated society.

Still, reading the Rule is one thing; living by it quite another. Our young novice, because he's young, wants things to happen in his life and the life of the community around him. But in a monastery change comes slowly. Tensions can rise and personal issues loom large.

If the novice enters the monastery wanting to be alone and holy, he finds out quickly how much reality can bite. First of all, it's hard to get up before six in the morning to pray, day in and day out. There's work to be done, too. The novice is often assigned monotonous tasks, like cleaning bathrooms or vacuuming. He might want to contemplate the sunset and write devotional poetry, but as in any home, dust collects, toilets and showers get dirty, and someone's got to do the dishes.

If the novice perseveres, he petitions the abbot to make his temporary vows, which are for three years. The chapter—the solemnly professed monks in the monastery—considers the petition. They pray and vote on the candidate by dropping balls (marbles) into a box. The marbles are colored white, black, and red. White is a "yes," red is "abstain," and black is "no." Thus, a novice may be "black-balled" (the phrase originated in the monastery) and not be allowed to profess first, or triennial, vows. If he's accepted, he'll make his vows and receive the monastic name and a new scapular and hood, symbolically dying to his old life. Three years later, he'll make his solemn profession of perpetual vows.

Even so, monks can be granted permission to leave the community, and some do, in their juniorate—the three years following triennial vows. There's nothing holding them except their vows. Like marriage, and even faith itself, living in a monastery is a continuing choice and surrender, an act of the will. Of course, desire and needs change. Faith can change, too. The ones who stay choose a life lived in community over other lives that might be lived.

Father Patrick Caveglia is one of the "60's monks," as I like to think of them. Their spirituality has been shaped by that time of social upheaval and the reforms of Vatican II. They are my closest friends and mentors in the monastery. If I were a novice at Conception Abbey, I'd want to be like these guys.

Fr. Patrick was a cradle Catholic. In college at Western Illinois University in the late 60's he got drawn into a deeper spiritual life. The civil rights movement deeply moved him and he came to see that one could make significant social change happen through being a priest. For him, social justice is a vital expression of Christian faith.

Fr. Patrick went to seminary at Conception, then decided to become a monk. But it wasn't social ideology that drew him into the monastery. Like Novice Andrew, he discovered the need for community and its importance in sustaining one's spiritual growth. At Conception Abbey he saw other monks of his generation living a life that was both intellectually challenging and spiritually nurturing. He wanted to be a part of that life.

His ambition was to go to graduate school and then become a priest. But life in a monastery is not about personal agendas. Abbot Kevin McGonigle answered Fr. Patrick's desire by assigning him to work in the kitchen instead, and then the Printery House, which manufactures and sells greeting cards and other gifts and is the Abbey's main source of revenue. Fr. Patrick worked there for the next twenty years—managing it for the last ten—before going to St. Louis for graduate studies and, eventually, the priesthood.

My Protestant soul rebels at the idea of a religious superior deciding the terms of my life. For Fr. Patrick, however, it was a necessary apprenticeship. He came to the monastery wanting personal fulfillment and became part of a community with its own needs. Carrying out the tasks he was assigned helped him come to know himself and discover gifts he didn't know he had. It made him a better priest when his call to orders came.

Standing here in the cemetery my gaze descends from the sky and brilliant leaves of the trees to the graves here on the west side of the sidewalk. I see the headstones of the monks buried here, nearly one hundred and fifty in all, with dates of monastic profession going all the way back to the nineteenth century and the days of Fr. Frowin Conrad, the founder of Conception Abbey.

In a few weeks, on November 2nd, the monks will celebrate All Souls with mass and a procession from the basilica out here to the cemetery, where their brothers are buried. Some names I recognize: Fr. Conrad. Fr. Alexis. Br. Aaron. Br. Leo. Br. Damian. Fr. Philip. I see the headstones of the older monks. They lived here long before my time, yet their names are familiar to me through the life of many stories.

There's Br. George Ernesti, who before he came to America and joined the monastery was drafted into the German Army and served in the trenches of WWI, but couldn't bring himself to shoot enemy soldiers; Fr. Dominic Lavan, a poet, singer, and fiddle player from County Mayo, Ireland, who helped found one of Conception's daughter houses; Brother Aloysius Stadelman, who cared for the apple orchard and made wine from grapes grown in the Abbey vineyard; Fr. Leo Gales, who chose the monastic life over a career in professional baseball; Br. Paschal Thanner, who crafted crucifixes and other statuary in his statue shop while a blue parakeet sang; and Fr. Eugene Howe, who said, on the night before he died, "it seems that God wants me now."[4]

In the third row back, in the shade of the maple near the south fence of the cemetery are the graves of Brother Stanislaus Thomas and Brother Roman Stahl. They had both come to Conception Abbey from North Dakota in the early twentieth century and were brothers in a community made up largely of priests.

Br. Stanislaus was a gifted musician despite an infection that had left him with punctured eardrums. He taught himself to play trumpet, trombone, and sax, and organized both a band and orchestra in the seminary. This was unusual, since at that time only priests held positions of leadership. He also served the monastery at various times as a cobbler, baker, janitor, porter, barber, and dining room attendant.

Br. Roman, who entered the monastery as a novice in 1928, was ten years younger than Stanislaus. He worked in the chicken yard of the Abbey farm, and later was refectorian, in charge of the monk's dining room. His sayings are part of Abbey lore: "There are three useless things: Rain falling on the ocean, the sun and moon shining in the sky at the same time, and preaching to monks."[5] Br. Roman was a great reader, despite his steadily deteriorating eyesight. He came to depend on recorded books for his reading. Ironically, then, Br. Roman, the reader, went blind; Br. Stanislaus, the musician, deaf.

Br. Stanislaus perhaps had the most difficult time of it. In Latin, the first word of the Rule is *obsculta*—listen. The inability to hear is more challenging for living in community, because many things don't get written down. Br. Stanislaus tended to get isolated, while Roman, despite his failing eyesight, was in the middle of things. Since he took care of the refectory, where the monks ate their meals, he heard all the news and gossip. "If you're going to lose a sense," Br. Roman would say in his heavy accent, "it's better to lose your sight than your hearing. I've got my talking books, but poor Br. Stanislaus can't hear what's going on."

The two monks were both eccentric, even more so as they got older. Living in a monastery has a way of sharpening personal singularities. "When I first came to the monastery," Br. Roman would often say, "There were all these *characters*, and then one by one the characters died, and I said, *where are all the characters?* Then I looked around and realized I had become one." He was a trickster and relished a good joke, sometimes taking it to diabolical lengths.

A crucifix hung on the wall near the dumb waiter in the monastic refectory. Because he was diabetic, Br. Stanislaus would frequently pass by this on his way to get at his sugarless jams and jellies in the refectory refrigerator. Whenever he did, he would "kiss the feet of Jesus," reaching out and touching the carven feet of the crucifix, then pressing his fingers to his lips. Br. Roman had the Abbey carpenter, Cletus Sullivan, raise the crucifix by an inch each week, until Br. Stanislaus, who was short, could no longer reach the feet of Jesus. "Ach!" he cried. "I think I'm *shrinking*, I'm *shrinking*!"

Br. Roman probably felt some remorse for this. On Br. Stanislaus' name day—a day of celebration in the life of a monk because it corresponds to the religious name given to him at the time of his monastic profession—Br. Roman said, "I feel like I should run over there and give him a big hug and a kiss, but I feel like such a hypocrite!" When Br. Stanislaus died in October of 1976, Br. Roman was deeply shocked.

Jean-Paul Sartre was partly right: other people can be hell on earth. But they can also be the path to the holy, and in their lives I've caught the unlooked-for glimpse of God. After Br. Roman died in 1981, he was buried here in St. Columba next to Br. Stanislaus and I can't help wondering if Br. Roman is still playing the trickster, and whether Br. Stanislaus has kissed the feet of Jesus himself.

Chapter Seven:
Crooked Lines

✣ ✣ ✣

I'm standing in a dark hallway. It is a few minutes after seven o'clock on a cold December morning in 1998, in the second week of Advent. All around me are monks. I can't see them very well, but I can hear their soft, steady breathing, interrupted occasionally by a quiet cough and the slight shuffle of feet, along with the creak and pop of the old oak floorboards underfoot. I catch the faint scent of mouthwash and after-shave lotion.

We are in *statio*, as the monks call it. We stand in quiet meditation before lauds, the second prayer office of the day. Since the basilica is presently under renovation and unusable, we will conduct the office in the chapter room. This room, which is located on the south side of the cloister, is both a meeting room for the monks and a chapel.

The monks are lined up in two rows, in order of seniority. This is set according to the date of their monastic profession, following the completion of the novitiate. I am in the left-hand column near the wall, just behind Br. Bernard. He's been shepherding me through my time here in the monastery.

When I arrived yesterday afternoon—Sunday—there was a light covering of snow on the ground. As I carried my small suitcase from my car to the front door of the monastery, Fr. Philip Schuster, the porter, came out on the front step. He held the front door open for me, welcoming me inside. For the next several days, with Abbot Gregory's permission, I would try to live the monastic life. This permission was not easily granted, and I was grateful to him for allowing me, a layperson, to enter into the monastic cloister.

My attention returns to the present moment. I'm not sure what I'm supposed to be doing. Preparing myself, I suppose. Is there a special monkish way to do that? I don't know. I ask God for help and wait with the others.

I was up around 5:30 this morning after a dream that I was about to have surgery and was waiting for the anesthesia. The first prayer Office, called vigils—formerly called matins—was at 6:00. That's early, but not so bad compared to how it was in the Middle Ages, when monks would rise at two o'clock in the morning to pray. This morning the monks chanted the Psalms *recto tono* ("on one note"). It's a musical minimalism that's both spiritual and practical: it encourages contemplation, and it's easier to perform early in the morning.

After vigils, I returned to my room on the second floor. Abbot Gregory has assigned me to Abbot Anselm's old room, on the west side of the monastery near the passage leading to the basilica towers, where the bells are rung. Anselm

Coppersmith was abbot in the 1960's and his former quarters are usually reserved for special guests of the monastery. It's a small suite, with its own sink and shower.

I had half-expected to be assigned to a regular room, where I'd have to use the community bathroom like the rest of the monks. I wouldn't have minded, but I'll take the convenience. Though it is no Trappist cell, the room is not lavishly furnished by any standard: The mattress is hard and the decor is plain. It reminds me of the college dorm rooms I lived in back in the seventies.

Settling into the straight-backed armchair next to my bed, I opened Augustine's *Confessions*. I brought this book for *lectio divina*, or "divine reading." It's a central part of monastic life. *Lectio* is often characterized as reading with the heart rather than the head, a way to listen to God by way of books. That's the way it's supposed to work, anyway. I fell asleep in my chair, waking just in time to hurry back downstairs for lauds.

We stand in silence. There will be no speaking to one another until after breakfast, which follows lauds. Suddenly, after some signal from the abbot that I miss, we begin to move down the hallway, turning into the chapter room, two by two. We walk toward the altar at the far end of the room between tiered sets of benches facing each other. This is the choir, where the monks sit. Before going to my place in the choir, I do what the other monks do and bow to the altar, then to the monk I have walked in with, Father Pascal. After all the monks have taken their places we begin the plainchant, led by the cantor.

Br. Frowin Reed is cantoring this morning. His monastic name comes from the founder of Conception Abbey, Fr. Frowin Conrad. Br. Frowin is a young monk, having just completed his novitiate in August. He stands on the other side of the choir and begins by singing the antiphon from Psalm 42: *Hope in God; for I shall again praise him, my help and my God.* We follow him, first one side of the choir and then the other, verse by verse:

Why are you cast down, my soul,
Why groan within me?
Hope in God; I will praise him yet again,
my savior and my God (Psalm 42:5)

The plainchant of lauds is more melodic than vigils. Other monasteries in the United States have moved toward reading out the Psalms; Conception continues the practice of plainchant. I'm glad. Even after only a short time in the monastery, I find its sound and rhythm entering my bones. It feels as though I am living inside a perfect fusion of word and music. I wonder: If I were really a monk and not merely a pretender, could I sustain this through weeks and months and years? Would it become a numbing routine, or a steady *basso continuo* sustaining the spiritual journey?

For a nester, an introvert, one drawn toward contemplation and a life of prayer in community, the monastic life would seem to be ideal. There is a part of me that is strongly attracted to this kind of life and what it can teach about the freedom that lies at the heart of obedience. Especially, I admire the stability of the monastic life. As Fr. Patrick has said to me, "we're always here." So they have been. In their prayer and presence, the monks of Conception Abbey have been an anchor for me through many storms.

Yet I can't idealize them. They are subject to the common temptations and faults that plague me. I have known them to lose their focus, grow weary of the daily round of duties in the monastery, chafe at the irritations and conflicts that are a feature of any close community, stumble over unexpected challenges and afflictions, cease listening to Christ of the Word. They are human beings, after all—pilgrims on a pilgrim's journey. By faith and the grace of God, they usually find their way back.

At mass in the chapter room later that day, a guest priest is presiding and we've reached that part of the mass following the consecration of the bread and the wine. The priest has come forward from the altar to distribute communion, along with two of the other monks who stand to either side with chalices full of wine. Here, once again, I stand on the outside looking in, feeling most like an outsider, a stranger.

Yet I still desire some kind of communion with them, even if it's only words of blessing. With some feeling of self-consciousness, I descend from the choir with the other monks in my turn. The priest stands there, distributing the wafers of consecrated bread to each monk as he approaches. When it's my turn, I cross my arms over my chest to refuse the Eucharist and ask the priest for a blessing. Before I can speak, he pops the wafer into my mouth.

I return to my place in the choir feeling stunned, like I'd just been given a treasure that I didn't expect. I'm happy—ecstatic, even. I also feel guilty, and more than a little puzzled. Somewhat furtively I glance around, wondering if anyone else noticed.

Later in the afternoon I encounter Fr. Hugh Tasch in the coffee room. A monk of Conception Abbey for almost fifty years, Fr. Hugh is white-bearded and somewhat frail. I appreciate his complex, dry wit and open, progressive spirituality.

He is also a talented keyboardist, with a gift for improvisation. At one of our employee Christmas parties, Marcel Rooney, who was abbot at the time, sang a tribute to the employees to the tune of "White Christmas." Fr. Hugh accompanied him on an electric piano, playing interludes of jazz improvisation after each verse that got so long and complex that at one point Abbot Marcel had to cut him short so he could finish singing the final verses of the song.

Today, Fr. Hugh is sitting at a table quietly reading a book. I get a cup of coffee from the coffee urn and am about to return to my room when Hugh says, almost to himself, as he turns the page of his books, "I couldn't help noticing that you received the Eucharist today."

So much for flying under the radar. With a slightly embarrassed look, I tell him that I had refused it. I set my coffee cup down on his table and cross my arms over my chest, as I had done at mass for the visiting priest. "That's what this means," I say.

"Oh," he said with a slightly amused smile. "I thought that was just some kind of pious Anglican prayer thing you were doing." Then he adds, with a slight shrug of his shoulders, "God draws straight with crooked lines." Then he returns to his book.

I have to agree with him, but as I return to my room upstairs I wonder what kind of picture God is drawing.

Vespers this evening begins the Solemnity of the Immaculate Conception. It's an important feast day for this monastery, which is named for the dogma defined by Pius IX in 1854, that Mary was conceived without the stain of original sin.

After vespers we gather for a banquet in the monastery refectory and the monks are seated according to seniority. I am next to Fr. Quentin Kathol, Br. Bernard, and Fr. Donald. Supper is normally a silent meal, with a monk reading aloud from a book selected for its informative or edifying quality. However, for feast days like today, the Abbot grants speaking privileges: He rings a small bell and says, "colloquamur," which means "let us speak." After this the monks respond, "deo gratias." Then, as food is served, we talk. There is bread, wine, and a main course of fish, rice and beans, and broccoli, with chocolate cheesecake for dessert. Afterwards, we clear the tables. I go to bed that night well satisfied.

The following day, Tuesday, the 8th of December, follows a Sunday schedule for the monks and students. Mass today is at 10:30 and there will be no classes in the seminary. It doesn't matter, since I am on sabbatical leave this semester and not teaching. In his homily at mass, Abbot Gregory speaks of Mary and her answer to the archangel, who has just announced to her that she will bear the Son of God: "Here am I, the servant of the Lord; let it be with me according to your word" (Luke 1:38).

Mary has been an ambiguous figure for Protestants. She is the mother of the Christ, but we're uncertain how to think of her, afraid of falling into idolatry. I remember the often-repeated claim that Catholics "worshiped Mary." But as I listen to the abbot's homily about Mary's willingness to do the strange, impossible thing that God has asked her to do, I realize that here is a portrait of true faith. She doesn't laugh, like Sarah had laughed when God declared that she, a woman of ninety, would bear a son. Mary has no inkling of what is in store for her, of how much future suffering she is taking on herself, yet she trusts God enough to surrender her body and life to him. I begin to understand why she is honored by Catholics, and why they pray to her.

After dinner, and before compline, Br. Frowin takes me on a tour through some of the backrooms of the monastery. He's excited, like a kid showing a guest around his parent's house. At this time, in December of 1998, Br. Frowin has been a monk for a year and a half. Before that he was a student of mine in the seminary and I had always appreciated his sardonic appraisals of life. It is plain to see how his life since joining the monastery has become more centered.

We head upstairs to the top floor. At present, no one lives in the rooms up here. Br. Frowin leads me through a maze of rooms stuffed with old books and other odds and ends, including a loom. He shows me a window where, he says—one corner of his mouth lifting in one of his wry smiles—he sometimes likes to climb out on the roof and look at the stars.

Br. Frowin says that he first wanted to be a part of the monastery because of prayer, liturgy, and learning. However, these reasons changed as his novitiate progressed. He found himself desiring to play his part in salvation, to offer obedience. He seems at peace with himself and with life, as if he had found himself. I keep thinking back to the abbot's homily. This appears to be the choice, for Br. Frowin as a monk, and for me: obedience to the need of the moment, the day, the year. It is surrender to someone we trust for the unknown future of our lives.

Compline that evening is quiet, reflective, even comforting. At the end of the office, the abbot sprinkles us with water from the aspergil. I don't understand what it means. Later, I am told that it is a night blessing and a hope that God will bring his work to completion in us. The sprinkled water is a sign of our baptism, which is also a sign of death—and resurrection.

Before leaving the monastery at the end of the week, I decide to visit my office. I think about the word "office," from the Latin *officium*: it denotes the times of prayer together in the monastery, which I have been part of for these past days. It is also this room with its desk and bookshelves and filing cabinets, where I prepare for my classes and meet with students. One is an act; the other, a place.

I feel strange being here: It's a little like stepping out of myself as I have been for the past week, a jarring re-entry into the atmosphere of my usual life. I sit at my desk and look around at the books on my shelves and the piles of paper on my desk. There is work here I need to do: The spring semester will begin in a few weeks and I have a couple of new classes to prepare for. But snow is beginning to fall outside my window and I want to go home to my wife and son.

What I have come to realize is that the seminary where I earn my living, though important to the life of this monastery, is not its reason for being. That is prayer, the inner work of monastic life. I like to think of the life of the monastery as a wheel, with the office—the daily chanting of the Psalms—and mass as the hub. These are the cries of the human heart, its loves and hates, its desires and deceptions and fears. Through them all is laid bare before God. So the Benedictine monks pray, and have prayed, for a millennium and a half. So I have prayed with them here.

When I pack my suitcase and take the road back home to my regular life I do so with a strange sense of longing for what I have left behind. The next morning in my own bed I awake early, before six, as if I were going to prepare myself for vigils.

Some months later, still riding the wave of this monastic enthusiasm, I become an oblate of Conception Abbey. I promise to live my life according to the Rule of St. Benedict, to the extent that I can as a layperson. It's a promise that is difficult to keep outside of the monastery, even teaching at a Catholic seminary in this quiet corner of the Midwest. And it will not protect me from what is coming. Yet it will be a reminder of where I have been, and what I have learned.

Chapter Eight:
Euthyphro

✤ ✤ ✤

As the monk comes into my office, he turns and, in Latin, commands the door to close behind him. When it doesn't, he laughs and closes it himself, then sits down in the chair near my desk where my students usually sit when they've come for help or consolation. But on this February afternoon, I am the student.

Father Isaac True looks small when he's sitting in a chair, but his stature looms large at Conception Seminary College. In my early years here I was always a little afraid of him. I think his intimidating reputation among the students infected me. His Socratic riddles have daunted seminarians for decades.

Today, Fr. Isaac seems unusually restless. He shifts around in the chair, flipping the scapular of his habit around like an oversized black tie. It may be his normal philosophical energy,

I suppose, or the fact that the straight-backed chair he's sitting in isn't as comfortable as he'd like.

Fr. Isaac has gray, thinning hair, and an impish smile. His face and voice are very calm, though he'll get more animated as he dives more deeply into the complexities of a subject. Always there is a sharp, driving Socratic edge to his teaching—and he is a born teacher—which never loses touch with his Benedictine hospitality. He'll tell you how you've missed half of the argument of a particular philosophical text, then smile and maybe even laugh a little. True to his name in Hebrew, laughter is never far away in Fr. Isaac. You know that for him, doing philosophy isn't about competition or destruction. It's about learning something worth knowing.

A couple of months earlier, I got the ambitious idea to do a tutorial with Fr. Isaac on ancient and medieval philosophy. For most people this sounds like asking to have a root canal for the fun of it, but I had my reasons: Philosophy has long been an interest of mine and I wanted to fill in some gaps in my knowledge. Years before I had learned philosophy in large lecture halls at the University of Wisconsin. Studying with Fr. Isaac, I thought, would give me a more Socratic experience. I also hoped it would help me answer a question that had long vexed me: what has philosophy to do with faith? Fr. Isaac agreed to my proposal and we began with Plato's dialogues.

Today's meeting is my second with the monk. A couple of weeks ago we discussed Plato's *Apology*, which recounts the trial of Socrates. He was condemned to death for impiety and corrupting the youth of Athens. Isaac explained that the dialogue, and indeed Socrates' whole life, was based upon the principle that it is always best to do good, even if it brings death upon you. For Socrates, doing good meant conducting tough-minded philosophical dialogues. Unfortunately, it also meant making some powerful enemies.

"Socrates' call to philosophy is a call to become a person like Socrates," Fr. Isaac said to me at that first meeting. "Someone who knows his limits, conducts himself with intellectual humility, knows when he's wrong, is a learner, and tries to help people to have the same kind of wisdom. For Socrates, the search for wisdom begins with critical thinking."

This is Fr. Isaac's conviction as well, and what he is known for here in the seminary: He's ever the Socratic gadfly. I like to think of him standing in front of class in his black Benedictine habit, gently skewering students with dialectic, encouraging them to think for themselves.

Each entering student at Conception Seminary College automatically becomes a philosophy major. Philosophy is considered central to priestly formation in the Catholic Church and has been for centuries. However, many of the students here take philosophy courses because they have to, not because they want to. Most come to appreciate it by the end of their years at Conception, but it's a tough road, especially in Fr. Isaac's classes. They would find it far easier to memorize a set of propositions, or learn a kind of Christian philosophy that substitutes ideology for intellectual rigor. But it's not what these seminarians need, as Fr. Isaac knows.

"I tell them that they can't possibly remain orthodox if they don't learn how to think critically," he says. "Convictions need critical thought."

Today Isaac and I are discussing the dialogue *Euthyphro*. Like the seminarians, Euthyphro, the main character, is a man of convictions. Socrates meets him on the steps of the courthouse where he's about to prosecute his own father for murder.

Euthyphro is absolutely convinced of the rightness of his position: "I say that the holy is what I am now doing," he declares to Socrates.[1]

Fr. Isaac begins, as usual, by asking me questions. Some I can answer. Mostly, though, I feel like I'm in a dark room and the monk is asking me to find things. Like students in my literature classes when they first encounter a poem, I'm looking for the master switch to turn on the light of knowledge. It's both difficult and exhilarating at the same time.

"What's the principle that Euthyphro built his life on?" Fr. Isaac asks me.

"Knowing the right thing to do," I answer.

This seems pretty obvious, but the monk turns the discussion in an unexpected and provocative direction.

"The holy," Fr. Isaac says. "Always do the holy." Then he adds, with a smile, "he's like a seminarian: Always do the holy thing."

"And Euthyphro knows what the holy thing is," I add.

"He claims that he does," Fr. Isaac says. "But does he really?"

I'm not sure about this. I've known many Euthyphros in my life. His name means "right thinker" and versions of him appear everywhere in the theatrical spectacle of American politics, both left and right. His voice is strong in our religious culture, too. Euthyphro is the zealot, the inquisitor, the ideologue; judge, jury, and prosecutor; an ungodly god-like man who is absolutely sure what is right and what is wrong. I know the character well because I have played his part: Looking like you're right all the time keeps other things at bay.

"What does Euthyphro actually do when he tries to live out his brand of holiness?" Fr. Isaac asks me.

"He prosecutes his father for murder."

"No," Fr. Isaac says at first, then pauses a moment, reconsidering. "Well, yes, that's true—but you find in the dialogue that he's telling the gods what is holy. He believes he knows better than they do, according to his sacred texts. Now what kind of religious offense is that?" Fr. Isaac doesn't wait for an answer. His blood is up now. "It's called *hubris*, a word that's usually translated as pride. Is there anything less holy for the Greeks than *hubris*?"

Fr. Isaac laughs. It's pure delight in the turn of the argument, the moment of enlightenment, the ironic revelation, the elegant denouement. He loves this stuff, loves thinking about it and teaching it.

"Practically speaking," he continues, his words coming out rapid-fire. "Euthyphro's effort to be holy has led him to unholiness. So if you build your life on a principle that you don't understand, you're very likely to commit a kind of moral suicide. For Socrates, this is worse than physical death. The only way you can escape hubris is by practicing Socratic ignorance."

Practicing ignorance. This is an intriguing idea to me. Many of my students achieve ignorance without any practice at all. Today, I feel like one of them.

"The only way to be truly honest," Isaac says, "is to admit your human limitations, because if you don't admit your human limitations you're making yourself a god."

This is especially difficult—the real challenge of the Socratic ideal, as far as I'm concerned. Persons do not like to admit their limitations, especially Americans. It makes us feel weak, impotent, at the mercy of larger forces. Of course we *are* at the mercy of larger forces, but we like to believe that we're in control of our lives, our futures.

We have been a country that believed it could do anything. Yet in recent times that belief has been severely challenged.

There are strong parallels between twenty-first century America and Athens in Plato's time: democracy under trial, war, vexing questions about leadership in an uncertain time, and the desire for eternal, changeless truths. Like them, we want strength and clarity. It's far more difficult to live with ambiguity, uncertainty, and unanswered questions.

"I don't believe that Plato was out to solve philosophical problems," Fr. Isaac says. "Instead, he was trying to create a very interesting discussion. And if you go deep enough, the discussion gets more and more interesting, and more and more complex, as you might have noticed. You keep discovering different layers in there, and each of the layers raises different issues. Of course, by Socratic ignorance—if he's really serious about all of this—Plato means that he doesn't have all the answers, and he gave us this tradition of philosophers not having all the answers." The monk pauses and says, with a smile and another infectious chuckle, "damn him."

Anybody might expect that the justification for teaching philosophy in a Catholic seminary is for buttressing answers that have already been decided, so that philosophy becomes a handmaiden to theology, a form of apologetics. Fr. Isaac doesn't teach it that way, and neither did Socrates. He wasn't out to defend the State or the status quo of religious institutions, but rather to serve the truth, wherever it led. A dangerous venture, as it turned out.

I used to think that people studied philosophy because they wanted to know the answers to the Big Questions. When we actually look into philosophical works like Plato's dialogues we discover that there aren't any—or, at least, there are very few. The dialogues are more literary drama than philosophical argument.

"There are four attempted definitions of the holy in the *Euthyphro*," Fr. Isaac points out. "The first two are Euthyphro's and the last two are Socrates'. He offers them to Euthyphro and shows that they don't work either." He pauses and then, with a mischievous smile, says. "Not even Socrates knows what is holy."

I think about this in relation to the seminary: "I suppose," I suggest, "that a seminarian might say to you, 'Well, Father, I know what the holy is because God has revealed that to me through the Church.' There would be things he would be quite sure of."

"That's why it's interesting to read the *Euthyphro* with the seminarians," Fr. Isaac says. "Their certainty gets shaken. It gets them thinking. I make that point repeatedly that they think they know it all, but how will they do when put to the test?"

Indeed. When I was nineteen or twenty, the monk's questions would have been very disturbing to me.

"He thinks he knows," Fr. Isaac says. "He thinks its objective. He doesn't want it to be a subjective thing."

"Right," I say. "He doesn't want to be a relativist."

Relativism is the notion that there are no absolute criteria for making moral judgments and so therefore all positions are equally valid.

"This is an illustration, you understand," Fr. Isaac says. "Socrates is doing right on the courthouse steps what they accuse him of doing: showing significant people in the community that they don't know what they're talking about, and humiliating them in public. Of course, there's no one there to watch him take Euthyphro apart, and Euthyphro is probably an imaginary figure. At least, I don't know anyone who would name his child 'right thinker.'" He laughs.

"He's a great character," I say, and he is, even though I also find him a self-righteous bastard, and a little too familiar for comfort. I appreciate the ending, too: Euthyphro can't stand it any longer and just wants to get out of there, as if he had looked at his watch and said, "wow, is that the time? Gotta go, Socrates."

The dialogue does have a happy ending: Euthyphro actually does the right thing and renounces his intention to prosecute his father. Socrates has saved him from the impiety of *hubris* by showing him his ignorance. That is, those who think they know it all are more likely to commit impiety than those who know their limitations and live by them.

Sometimes I ask my students what they think philosophy is for. What is its purpose? There are many possible answers to this question: Philosophy is concerned—or should be concerned—with the clarification of meaning, of language; or, it should focus on the search for truth, a quest for life's meaning and purpose; or it is for defending religious orthodoxy and attacking heresy.

The German philosopher Martin Heidegger said that the purpose of philosophy is to make things more difficult.[2] Certainly philosophy may reinforce a kind of right thinking, a dogmatic narrowness, but it can also entangle us in difficulties, problems, a maze of misdirection. This isn't necessarily a bad thing, as Socrates knew: It may lead us to wisdom and humility, and realism about the human condition.

Yet it is one thing to play with these ideas in the classroom and quite another to wrestle with them when the stakes are higher. When faith itself is in question, for instance. If there is a philosophical road to wisdom it leads through a forest where the clearings are few and the shadows are perplexing. It is a negative way, as I have discovered, and it's easy to get lost there.

Chapter Nine:
The Woods

❖ ❖ ❖

My faith didn't disappear like Reverend Clarence Wilmot's does in the opening pages of John Updike's novel *In the Beauty of the Lilies*, as "a set of dark sparkling bubbles escaping upward."[1] It was more like the collapse of a rotted-out house under the pressure of strong, cold winds.

It had taken time for the rot to do its work. Years, in fact. Yet there is always a tipping point, a final straw. Mine was philosophical. In the winter of 2002 a colleague had asked me to comment on an article he had written, a presentation of rationalistic, proposition-based religious belief. His argument was earnest and forthright, but I found it unconvincing. I remember thinking: *this isn't my faith*.

Then, unexpectedly, the question boomeranged: *what is my faith?* The question seemed to come from the outside and I found that I couldn't answer it—at least, not with what I had muddled along with up to now: a hash of vague, half-baked arguments and a faint and elusive pattern of experience that, if interpreted in a certain way, is evidence of a sort. But it was very thin.

Suddenly, the philosophical specter of Immanuel Kant rose from my graduate school days. I had taken a course on Modern Philosophy at Wisconsin as part of a doctoral minor in philosophy. The philosophy of Immanuel Kant was the culmination of that course. Kant is the famous German philosopher from the late eighteenth century who argued that we can have no direct sensory apprehension of the Thing-in-itself, the numinous, beyond all sensory experience. For Kant, God remains a transcendental ideal, a necessary condition of human existence, but there is no way to know him directly or to prove that he exists (or doesn't exist).

I know that I'm summarizing (and poorly at that) only a fragment of Kant's full argument in the *Critique of Pure Reason*, which, if one accepts Kant's premises, is a beauty, representing a watershed in modern philosophy. Kant boasted that he had made faith possible in a world of scientific reason. For me, unfortunately, his argument was the final blow to faith. I didn't want God as a transcendental ideal, a necessary premise in a bloodless argument; I wanted him tangible and real—and *knowable*.

Kant seemed finally to make clear to me the absurdity of faith. Prior to this, I would have said that for the past twenty-eight years I had known God. Now, with the mere movement of my pen, God had become "God." The quotation marks expressed it: God was a noun, a mere word. I felt the intellectual absurdity of trusting in an abstraction.

This is a pretty nerdy way to lose one's faith, I know: "God isn't there anymore—let's see. . . yes, I read about that once in

Kant." Not long after that, a seminarian was telling me with comfortable satisfaction how he could "prove God's existence." I smiled a cynical smile, thinking, *yeah, heard that one before.* For me, philosophy had become a devouring worm hollowing out the last supports of my faith. Or so I believed.

Thinking back on that time, I understand now that Kant's philosophy had only given me the intellectual proof text for a deeper problem, one much deeper than rational thought. I wondered if Immanuel Kant, a devout Lutheran, had experienced the same problem as I did. Was his argument a way of digging himself out of the agnostic hole that Isaac Newton and David Hume had put him in?

I've heard it said that theology is a form of autobiography, a telling of the personal through the form of the abstract. I think that to some extent philosophy has the same character. Rather than some oracular pronouncement of definitive answers, I prefer to see philosophy as an elusive, troubling gadfly, like Socrates on the courthouse steps in Athens, puzzling out what it means to be holy and unable to come up with a definite answer to the question. This may be a deficiency or a blessing; I haven't yet decided which.

Dante's *Divine Comedy* begins with the most famous mid-life crisis in literature. A man—the poet Dante—in his middle years, loses his way in a dark wood, a sign of his moral and spiritual confusion and error. Where I come from in northern Minnesota, the woods are dark and deep, a dense tangle of branch and leaf where you can't see more than ten feet in front of you. That's where I was now: lost in the deep woods.

It wasn't really Kant who had put me there. My brother had: a final legacy—and gift, I would eventually come to see—of his sudden death less than a year before. The grief of loss had coursed through my emotional life like a strong, underground river, finding its way to the surface along unexpected faults and rills. It left me drifting and vulnerable, drowning wisdom in a flood of emotional impulse. I was confronting my own mortality. Death had ceased being an abstraction and had become *my* death.

Dealing with his death meant dealing with the distance there had always been between Kurt and me as brothers. Dealing with the fact that he was gay and I hadn't known it, and even after I did know it, or thought I did, we still didn't talk about it. Perhaps it was because there were things about his life that Kurt had held secret and these had never been told because in families there are unwritten rules about what's talked about and what isn't and, whether out of fear or embarrassment, I couldn't bring myself to violate the rules, and now it was too late. He was dead. My grief was sharpened by regret over the silence left between us.

What did Kurt's death have to do with my loss of faith? I don't know. The human heart doesn't work out these things like an algebraic equation. I didn't blame God for it. But there it was: my existence had become a nothingness, a bleak, wintery landscape. I had lost my faith and I didn't know where or how. It didn't even seem to be a choice on my part, only a waking up to a different reality in which God seemed very distant.

In my younger years as an evangelical I would have denied that such a thing could happen to a believer, a born-again Christian. Once saved, always saved, we used to say with smug assurance. If you give your life to Jesus—if you truly, sincerely ask him into your heart—he'll never leave you. On the other hand, if you say you lost your faith, then you never had it to begin with.

But I did, or at least I thought I did. The beginning of my conscious journey of faith came in my junior year of high school and I was sixteen. I can still vividly recall the excitement and promise of that time. It was youthful, emotional, but very real to me. I had been invited with a bunch of my friends to a church in a nearby town to watch a movie entitled *A Thief in the Night*. It was about the Rapture, the sudden removal to heaven of all Christian believers on the eve of the Tribulation, a worldwide apocalypse culminating in the Second Coming of Christ. The film scared the hell out of me. I was afraid of being left behind. That night—May 5th, 1974—I gave my life to Christ, or as much of life as a teenager could give.

The date is important. A born-again Christian—even a back-sliding one like me—can usually give it to you. It's a new beginning, a more authentic baptism, as I believed then. I had been baptized as an infant, but within evangelical Protestantism this counted for nothing. If you were to become a child of God, it would have to be by your own choice, the prayer you pray to God, asking him into your life (as if he weren't there before). Your baptism came afterword, a profession to the world that you were born again.

In orthodox theological terms, this resembles the heresy known as semi-Pelagianism, which asserts that instead of being a gift, faith only follows our choice. I didn't know this at the time and even now when I do know it, I can't help think in the true Protestant spirit, *so what?* God calls us to him, and we come by many paths, even through watching cheesy apocalyptic thrillers like *A Thief in the Night*, when conversion is driven by adolescent need and a fear of death, and I loved God the way one might love a good insurance policy.

Still, one has to begin somewhere. This brand of religion was certainly more exciting than confirmation classes at the

Methodist Church, where each week the elderly pastor showed us slides of his trip to the Holy Land. In those early days I became intoxicated with the idea of the End Times and prophecy. We were reading Hal Lindsey's apocalyptic fantasy *Late Great Planet Earth* with hungry fascination. I felt part of something serious and important. Faith was a hormone-charged adolescent high, like the erotic rush of new love.

By the time I entered college I wanted to be an intellectual Christian, someone with all the answers. I was heavily into apologetics—the defense of the Christian faith—and was reading evangelical heavy-hitters like C. S. Lewis, Francis Schaeffer and Os Guinness. Beneath this intense program of intellectual discovery I was going through the usual post-adolescent struggle for identity, as well as my own latent doubts, though I didn't understand that then. I wanted to prove the truth of this strange, unworldly, absurd belief in a man who claimed to be God, but even more desperately than this I wanted to prove that I was worth something to others.

But college exposed me to other books and ideas that didn't fit the neat evangelical categories. I began to compartmentalize my thinking: on the one hand, I lived the part of the devoted Christian who attended the college Intervarsity Christian Fellowship meetings every Thursday night; on the other, I harbored a secret life as a skeptical, would-be intellectual who got his kicks from reading Albert Camus and Friedrich Nietzsche. The two streams ran side by side all the way through college and graduate school. They continue to flow through my life.

Now, over twenty years later, I was no longer sure what faith meant. It was as if I had lost the very meaning of the word. Was it something I felt? Or was it something I did? Or was it something I knew?

At first I sought answers in books. I read Paul Tillich's *The Dynamics of Faith*. Tillich characterizes faith as "the state of being ultimately concerned." Faith is both rational and nonrational, he says. It's about freedom, and choice and, above all, passion—a concern that rises above other concerns.[2]

Moreover, faith, says Tillich, lives in uncertainty. Because of its nature as concern, doubt must be a part of it, simply because faith is always a risk. It is dynamic, always moving, rather than a set of propositions one believes in or a feeling one has to somehow sustain. Doubt, Tillich says, is a confirmation of faith because it indicates how serious the concern is.[3]

Well, that sounded good, but my problem wasn't doubt, exactly. It seemed deeper than that.

One day over lunch in Kansas City I asked Linda Yeager, a deacon in the Episcopal Church and one of my closest friends, what faith was.

"Surrender," she answered promptly. "It's a choice, but it's a choice to let go."

"I don't think I can do that," I said.

"That's because you don't trust God."

I looked across the table at her. There was no hiding it, not with her: We'd been friends for too long.

"No, I don't," I said, feeling at the same time both how true it was, and how awful. It was a confession, but also in some way a claim of freedom.

I couldn't help wondering if this was what happened when a marriage went bad. I didn't know. Carolyn and I had been happily married for twenty years. How did that work? How did I keep surrendering to her? Trusting her? Because I always had? In the same way, was faith in God a continuing choice, or a comfortable habit? And if it were mere habit, a comforting security against the fear of death, wasn't it time to face up to it and walk away?

But I didn't want to. Not really. Oh, there were days when I felt strong, braced against the abyss. But most of the time I was depressed. I wanted to believe. I think I've got a "belief gene." Perhaps it's a gift of grace, but I find it hard not to believe in God. Call it Pascal's God-shaped emptiness or Augustine's restless heart, never resting until it rests in God, I couldn't be an agnostic for long, much less an atheist. Whether because of weakness or strength, God was a part of me. Yet I didn't trust him. It was an awful position to be in.

"The surrender will come when you hit bottom," Linda said.

When would that happen? I wondered.

My conversation with Linda took place on Friday, June 7th. I had no idea what was in store for me or for others I loved three days later.

Chapter Ten:
The Stranger

✤ ✤ ✤

That Monday morning, June 10th, 2002, dawned warm and cloudy over the green hills and valleys surrounding Conception Abbey. At around 8:30 that morning Brother Michael Marcotte was on his way to his day's work designing greeting cards at the Printery House, located across the parking lot, east of the basilica. He saw a man who had just pulled into the parking lot on the west side of the basilica in a green Chevy Cavalier. Br. Michael gave the man a friendly wave and continued on his way.

About this same time Fr. Patrick Caveglia had left his office in the monastery where he managed the business affairs of the abbey. It was a slow Monday morning, warm and muggy. The treasurer, Brother Jacob, was on vacation, and there wasn't a lot to do in the office. He'd had a weekend assignment at a parish near Kirksville, on the other side of the state, and was still a little tired from the long drive. He decided to walk over to the library to drop off a magazine.

Fr. Patrick decided not to take his usual route through the monastery and basilica and walked outside instead. If he had, he would have come face to face with a short, thin, 71-year old man named Lloyd Jeffress now walking slowly through the basilica toward the door into the monastery with a .22 rifle slung over his shoulder and an assault rifle in his hands.

In the library, Patrick brought the journal back to the workroom, then stopped at the magazine table on his way out and picked up the latest *New Yorker*, settling into one of the leather upholstered chairs to read the cartoons. This probably saved his life. Not long afterward he made his way back toward his office, walking through the east end of the basilica, behind the altar, and into the monastery. He didn't know it, but he was following the same route Jeffress had just taken less than fifteen minutes before.

He walked down the Glass Hallway. Through its large windows, which face into the monastery courtyard, he could see the flowers that Brother Damian Larson had been watering only minutes earlier. The courtyard was empty now.

Fr. Patrick came through another door into the south hallway, the hub of the monastery. Opening off this hallway are the chapter room, the refectory, the coffee room, and at the far end, the business office. There, on the wooden floor in front of him, lay Br. Damian. He was dressed in his work clothes. Fr. Patrick saw blood at his mouth and thought Br. Damian had collapsed from some kind of internal hemorrhage. After saying a short absolution over the dead monk, he hurried down the hallway and into the coffee room to call 911 on the telephone there.

In the room he found two more monks lying on the floor: Fathers Kenneth Reichert and Norbert Schappler. There was blood everywhere. They had both been shot, but were still alive. Fr. Norbert had managed to crawl to the phone and call 911. "You've got to get help," Fr. Kenneth told Fr. Patrick.

Fr. Patrick ran toward his office. As he reached the end of the south hallway he looked to his right and saw Father Philip Schuster lying, face down in his own blood, in the west hallway which runs back toward the basilica. Fr. Philip had evidently come from the porter's office when he heard the shots down the hallway. Lloyd Jeffress, who had come around the corner, had shot him once as the monk ran up and, after Philip fell, shot him again in the back of the head. As he had done with Br. Damian, Fr. Patrick absolved him in the name of the Father, the Son, and the Holy Spirit.

The horror was becoming unimaginable. In his office Fr. Patrick tried calling 911, but all the lines were busy. "What do I do now?" he said aloud, over and over in the empty room.

Leaving his office, Fr. Patrick stepped back into the hallway where the bodies of Fr. Philip and Br. Damian lay. It was eerily quiet. *Who could have done this?* he thought *And where was the shooter? Was he still in the building?* He knew he had to get out. He decided to head toward the Infirmary, a building south of the monastery where the ill and elderly monks resided. It had doors that could be locked. Once there, he waited for the police.

That morning had begun for me at my favorite haunt in Maryville: a coffee shop on Main Street. It was still the beginning of summer and I was enjoying my break from teaching. Ironically, that morning I was editing the manuscript of a murder mystery I had written and hoped to get published (I never did). The story was set at a Benedictine abbey.

Around nine I went home, but I wasn't there more than a few minutes when I got a call from a friend who told me that she had heard from a neighbor with a police band radio that there had been shootings at Conception Abbey.

I hung up the phone and sat staring out the back window of our house. What I had just heard sounded incredible. Shootings at the abbey? A few minutes later I called my wife and told her the news.

"I think I'm going out there," I said.

She wasn't happy about the decision: "You're going to do *what?*"

If I had thought it through more deliberately, I would have probably stayed home. Yet I wasn't thinking, only feeling. It wasn't about seeking thrills or danger. It wasn't about me at all. It was about the monks.

"I have to go," I pleaded with her. "It might be some kind of mistake but I've got to check it out. I'll be careful."

There was an unreality to things as I drove down the south strip of Maryville, past McDonald's and Wal-mart. It felt as if the world had changed. Nothing looked quite the same, quite as *ordinary* and peaceful. It was similar to the feeling I had on 9/11, only nine months before, except stronger. This was immediate and near, rather than a distant television event. I felt like I was *alongside myself* in the car, driving yet also standing outside of the moment, watching everything with the eyes of a stranger. Yet I hoped it was all some kind of horrible mistake.

I drove south of town, the way I usually do, turning east on the county road five miles south of Maryville. Past the small hamlet of Arkoe the road rises out of the Hundred and Two River valley over a set of steep ridges. I had just crested the second of these when I saw an ambulance approaching me, coming fast down the farther hill, its lights flashing. All hope that this was some kind of mistake disappeared. I didn't know it at the time, but inside the ambulance was Fr. Kenneth Reichert, shot in the leg and abdomen. He was on his way to St. Francis Hospital in Maryville.

Five minutes later I came up the last ridge and into Conception. Ahead of me the road was blocked by a couple of pickup trucks. A small group of men stood looking toward the twin towers of the basilica. When I asked if I could go on to the abbey the men near the pickup refused. "We're not letting anyone through," one of them said to me with authoritative bluntness.

I didn't want to return home and I couldn't stay where I was, so I got back in my car and turned down a gravel side street that took me to Lance Richey's house, just north of St. Columba Cemetery, which lay between it and the abbey. Lance was a colleague of mine in the seminary back then. Together, we stood in his front yard and waited.

There wasn't much news to hear yet, except that monks had been shot and some were dead. There were no names either. One monk—Fr. Norbert, I later learned—had been flown to Heartland Hospital in St. Joseph, and another taken out by ambulance. Employees were leaving the abbey grounds one by one in their cars. The police were going room to room throughout the abbey, evacuating monks, guests, and staff. They were also looking for the shooter or shooters—they weren't sure how many there were.

As I stood on Lance's front lawn, looking south over the trees of the cemetery toward the basilica towers, I realized that though the road was cordoned off to traffic, I could walk through the cemetery to where I knew the monks would probably be gathered on the far side.

I also realized what going to them would mean for me. Beyond questions and answers, doubt and faith, I would be choosing to embrace a more intimate suffering. It was a leap, but not one of faith. I couldn't see God in this tragedy; I couldn't see him anywhere today. Rather, it was love that drew me.

I harbored no illusion that I could offer comfort to anyone, least of all the monks. This was their tragedy, their loss. I only worked for them. Yet such is the way of things that Conception Abbey had become more than a workplace to me, and the monks more than employers. I wanted to be there with them, who had supported me these past twelve years. Perhaps what I instinctively sought was comfort and assurance that their world of faith wasn't coming apart like mine had in the face of death. So I walked into the cemetery.

On the south side, on a grassy slope between the wrought-iron fence and the county road that runs past the abbey, I found most of the monks who had been evacuated from the monastery. They were sitting, waiting for news. Their faces were tense, their eyes strained, haunted. Some were in tears.

I sat with them. There wasn't much else to do. Across the road I saw a tangled mass of emergency vehicles with strobing red and blue lights. A helicopter circled overhead. There were serious-looking men in uniforms and body armor, carrying all manner of weaponry. It was a surreal transformation of this peaceful, bucolic setting. I saw Fr. Patrick, talked to him for a few minutes. I was grateful to see him still alive.

Not long afterward we heard that they had located the body of the shooter in a pew at the back of the basilica. After walking through the first floor of the monastery, shooting whoever he encountered, he had committed suicide there, putting the muzzle of the Ruger .22 into his mouth and pulling the trigger. Later, Abbot Gregory came out and spoke to us, telling us who had been shot and who had been killed. He was composed, almost supernaturally calm. Only those that knew him well could see the strain he was under. Then he went and spoke to the news media gathered in the field west of the cemetery, telling those in the world who were listening that the monks of Conception would not be led by fear.

An hour later I left, walking back through the cemetery, past the graves of the monks. Soon there would be two more added to their company, buried like the others in plain pine caskets. On the way home I called my mother in northern Minnesota to tell her what had happened. She had already heard about it on the radio. It was on network news that evening, with Peter Jennings talking about the shooting over a helicopter shot of the abbey. By the next day, the story had disappeared from television. For the news media it was on to the next thing. But here in northwest Missouri it was not soon forgotten.

That afternoon I sat in a lawn chair in my back yard and stared at the house across the alley and the clouds breaking above it, moving across the Missouri sky on a light summer wind. I didn't know what to feel. My wife came home from work that afternoon and stayed with me. We talked about Br. Damian, Fr. Kenneth, and the others. Later, I called Linda Yeager. I told her that God had betrayed the monks.

"No he didn't," Linda said. "The shooter did."

I listened, unconvinced.

"You have to suffer because you love the monks," Linda said. The thing is, I knew this was true. I had known it since I decided to walk through the cemetery. Love meant suffering, a truth of our world that I was finding hard to bear. If God were somewhere in all of this, sitting back paring his fingernails, I wanted nothing to do with him.

"It's alright for you not to believe," Linda said. It took a friend, and someone with deep trust in God, to tell me that. She knew I'd have to find my own way back, and she knew it wouldn't be easy for me, if I made it at all.

I told her about Abbot Gregory and how he had been a center of peace and self-control on a day of grief and horror.

"You watch him," Linda said. "You watch the monks."

The wounds they had suffered were deep. Lloyd Jeffress had violated the sanctity and peace of the monastery, their home, with extreme violence. It haunted them. For a long time after the shootings Fr. Patrick would see the shadow of Fr. Philip's body in the west hallway; he would avoid walking over the place where Br. Damian had lain. He told me that he would never forget the smell of the blood. Father Xavier Nacke wondered, whenever the front door of the basilica opened during prayer, was this another shooter coming to kill? Norb Scheiber, the abbey carpenter who made the plain pine coffins for the dead monks, carefully scrutinized cars that entered the abbey grounds past the windows of his workshop.

Yet healing had begun. Over a thousand people came to pay their last respects to Br. Damian and Fr. Philip. The monks were surprised at the response to the tragedy, at how much they had touched people's lives. Fr. Kenneth, during his time in the hospital recovering from his gunshot wounds, received over five hundred cards. His room was filled with flowers from well-wishers.

That summer, Fr. Patrick was out serving in parishes frequently while Fr Kenneth and Fr. Norbert recovered. The gospel readings that summer came from Matthew and he learned that that gospel talks a lot more about forgiveness and reconciliation than he had realized. Fr. Patrick was also hearing a lot of confessions concerning forgiveness. He realized that Br. Damian and Fr. Philip were affecting change in people's lives. He recognized grace, mysterious and unexpected.

In his homily at the funeral mass for Br. Damian and Fr. Philip on the Friday following the shootings, Abbot Gregory said that when "brutal deeds are enacted, it calls for heroic and radical forgiveness."[1] This is not the way of the world. We want to dispense retribution, not forgiveness, whether with hard words, or bullets, or cruise missiles. If we've been hurt, betrayed, violated, it's far easier and more natural to hate our enemy. It's true that Christ forgave his executioners, but that was the Son of God, not us. Forgiveness is a difficult labor, an act of the will; like prayer, a discipline. It can take years, even a lifetime.

Still, I have talked to others at the abbey who think the cost too high for the benefit. These were two men who, it could be said, were ready for death. Fr. Philip often said that he was prepared to die. But what of all the other innocent deaths, such as the Amish children in Nickel Mines, bound hand and foot before they were executed?

The monks will say that they don't know why Br. Damian and Fr. Philip died. God has not revealed any ultimate purpose. This is never a very satisfying answer for those who seek answers, especially when grief and anger are still raw.

It is a great mystery—even a great absurdity, perhaps—to believe, to have faith in the face of evil. Surrender takes a broken heart but sometimes that isn't enough. It wasn't for me—not for another two years. The shootings seemed a confirmation of what I already felt: that faith in such an arrangement of things, in an Author that wrote this particularly malevolent play we call Life, seemed impossible to accept. Indeed, that God was not great. When Linda said I would have to hit bottom, she wasn't kidding.

Yet, even when I couldn't trust God, I could trust the monks.

Chapter Eleven:
Passages

✥ ✥ ✥

At its best, writing brings illumination. This is what I teach my students in my classes at the seminary: write to know and be known. Writing is also a gift. What do we give? Only what we have.

In the months after my loss of faith and even before the shootings it seemed important to me to write down what was happening to me. I didn't understand it, nor did I sense any kind of purpose in what I was experiencing. But I wrote. It seemed to me then only an act of personal transparency, that if I were going to make something of what had happened, I would need these marks upon a page to allow me to throw some light upon my life. It was a gift to myself.

In my literature classes at Conception Seminary College I have taught many stories of the quest, that mystery-haunted archetype of life's journey. It is an age-old story that seems never to wear itself out no matter how many times it's told and retold, such as in the many versions of the Grail Quest, or in Sir Gawain's temptation-ridden journey to the Green Chapel and his deadly confrontation with the Green Knight. In more recent versions, there is Frodo and Sam's forlorn trudge to Mount Doom in *The Lord of the Rings* and Harry Potter's final, dangerous quest for the horcruxes that will enable him to triumph over Voldemort.

The medieval knight in search of adventure was called a knight errant. That last word—"errant"—is a curious one. In *Blue Highways*, his very personal quest-story disguised as a travel book, William Least-Heat Moon points out that its etymological root is the word "erren," a Middle-English word that means "'to wander about.'"[1] The word comes from the Latin "erro, errare" and is, of course, the root of the English word "error." To wander, then, is to make mistakes, to be "in error." The knight errant is thus the knight error-maker, the knight failure.

Yet through failure the knight achieves the quest, which may be what he doesn't expect. Such errant wanderings bring us, humiliated and broken, to the edge of what we know, and even beyond, to the place of unknowing. Such are the rough passages of *la vita nuova*—the New Life.

It is late June, two weeks after the shootings at Conception Abbey, and I am in Delavan, Wisconsin with Carolyn and Peter. We are attending our niece's wedding here and are staying with Bill and Linda Myrick. Bill was the former associate rector of Grace Episcopal Church in Madison, which we attended back in graduate school days. Now he pastors an Episcopal church here in Delavan.

I remember the first time we talked to him: we had him over to our apartment when we were considering joining the Episcopal Church. At the time we were troubled by the idea of infant baptism. Evangelicalism had taught us that the only authentic baptism was "believer baptism" at an age when the person could fully understand what she was doing. We were wrestling with the concept, especially because we were planning on having children as soon as we could. "I don't understand it," I said in some frustration. I've never forgotten what Bill said very quietly in reply to me: "I'm not sure I understand it either." I think that was the moment when I knew I could be an Episcopalian.

Bill had shepherded us into the Episcopal Church and we were close friends, but here, this weekend, after all that has happened, I choose not to talk to him about my loss of faith. He knows I'm having problems—Carolyn wrote to him about them—but I know he won't broach the subject unless I do first. Instead, I enjoy his hospitality and listen to him, to the talk about church and faith and spirituality. Still, I can't help but feel disconnected from this talk, much as I felt during the wake for the slain monks a couple of weeks ago.

It was a beautiful, moving service, but I found that I couldn't sing the songs or chant the responses or pray the prayers. Yet it brought comfort to me somehow because of the love I have for the monks and the way they live, of all that they have taught me. But the trust in God isn't there any longer and I wonder now if it will ever return. I wonder, too, if I desire it to return or even if I can ever care again. I don't know.

It helps me to watch Bill and what he does as a priest and friend. He displays a faith that is straightforward and loving, real and unpretentious. He reminds me of the monks.

There may be other causes, other motives for what has happened to me. Human beings are complicated emotional creatures, for all our talk of reason and discipline. We hardly know ourselves even in the best of times. Perhaps, after all, I am only hiding with my little bag of stolen goods. One of the key truths I cling to is my understanding of my own shortcomings. Maybe it's because I grew up in Minnesota, where thinking too well of oneself runs counter to the grain of life.

It is late August. I am standing on a hill under the thick, broad branches of a white oak tree. The Missouri landscape of farm field and copses of trees rolls out west, away from me toward farther hills, ever westward toward Nebraska. The morning is warm and humidity still pools like heavy mist in the hollows between the ridges. All around me are gravestones. I read the names carved into them: Parshall, Logan, Palmer, Rodman.

I discovered Quitman Cemetery by accident. I like driving the county roads through the small Missouri hamlets: Parnell, Skidmore, Pumpkin Center, Toad Hollow. As I passed through the town of Quitman one day the road fell away into a curving dip and I glimpsed an airy rise to my right and gravestones under broad, shady trees. Turning up a gravel road I parked in the shade of the trees, letting the silence of Sunday fall over me.

It's not that I have an obsession with cemeteries, but on most Sunday mornings Quitman feels especially peaceful, a place for me to come and be alone. The dead are quiet beneath stone, grass, and root. They give me space to be who I am without illusions. Like the St. Columba Cemetery near the abbey, this is a communion of saints in the general human sense. I am encircled by those who have lived and loved—and perhaps believed in something beyond this life. This place is more about life than death to me. There is hope here that living is not in vain.

I can't say that I'm at peace here on this particular morning at Quitman. I feel unusually restless, a child at the door of God's presence, yet unable to speak, like the children at the gate in T.S. Eliot's purgatorial poem, *Ash Wednesday*, who will not go away, but who at the same time are unable to pray.[2]

Still, this place is my church, in a time when I can't bring myself to go to the church my family has attended since we came to Maryville twelve years ago. This has made Sunday morning both the worst and the best time of the week for me now. Worst because of the alienation I feel; best, because as Paul Tillich might put it, my concern is most keen. Is this faith? This doubt and double-mindedness?

Thinking of Tillich, I remember what he says about the necessity of doubt in faith, that it in fact confirms faith. Does it confirm my faith here, now? This morning, amidst the fields and far ridges and the blue Missouri sky over me I have a sense of something there, yet what is it? I have been feeling this more strongly lately, but I don't know what to do about it, this longing I feel.

It came on me as I was driving here, a silent question: *will you surrender, and continue to surrender, to Me? Do I have your love?* I didn't know how to answer. I could have said "yes," but it would have been, I'm afraid, only a means of getting the burden off me, of going back, of being comfortable again. I want to believe God is speaking to me, but I've long been so skeptical of that kind of thing that believing in it now is impossible. Yet the echo of the question lingers.

I have been reading other scriptures out of some impulse to be fair and open-minded about all of this, as if I could somehow step out of the Christianity I have been immersed in most of my adult life. I have read *The Koran*, the *Bhagavad-gita*, books on Zen Buddhism. They're interesting and provocative, even illuminating at times, but they don't capture me like the Bible does—especially the Old Testament, with its incomparable poetry and stories of characters unforgettable and strange enough to be real.

Autumn has begun and with it another school year commences. In the monastery I talk to Fr. Patrick, my spiritual director, about losing my faith. This is what I appreciate about the monks: you can tell them almost anything and they don't flinch or draw back, or get defensive. He listens and we talk some more. He tells me to stay in the company of people of faith, if I am indeed serious about wanting to return. "God will speak to you through these people." Does that mean I have to go to church? I don't voice the question but Fr. Patrick gives me an answer anyway: be with people of faith wherever you find them, in church or outside.

A couple of weeks later I talk to Abbot Gregory. He has been my friend for years and when I meet him—the first time we have talked together since the shootings—I can't help remembering the morning of June 10th when he came out and told us which monks had been shot by Lloyd Jeffress. Who was dead; who was living. He was a rock of faith and forgiveness that day, even in the midst of shock and grief. On that day he became for me, as for many others who saw him, an indelible image of Benedictine grace and peace.

Now his steady green eyes study me closely as I tell him that I have lost my faith and haven't been to church in over six months. My wife and son have attended, but I've stayed home or driven out to Quitman. There is no shock in his face, no reprimand, only a slight frown that tells of his concern for me.

Talking in a gently measured yet firm voice, as he might talk to an erring novice monk, he says that at times the head and heart must follow the body. In other words, go to church with your family and fake it 'til you make it. I might dismiss this admonition if it were coming from anyone but Abbot Gregory. He's been there for me at key points in my life and I trust his insights and advice, because he doesn't give it lightly. He is, indeed, Father Abbot to this confused and stumbling oblate.

I am praying. It is the first prayer I have uttered in many months. The prayer isn't coherent, only something broken, which begins, "I'm not sure about this—" It isn't much, but at least it's a start and the best I can do right now. I have a vague feeling that maybe the angels are rejoicing, but I can't seem to take my relative importance in the world that seriously.

One part of my mind desires to know and be known by God, to have him fill the space inside that is empty; the other side laughs at the idea. Right now, plain emotional need is moving me and I have returned to church with my family, though I do not attend every week. Carolyn has been patient and understanding with me while I've been absent from her on Sunday mornings, but I know it's a strain on her. For the first time in our marriage, we are on seriously divergent paths. Peter doesn't understand, but is afraid, I think, to ask me what is wrong.

I feel quite tentative and uneasy about it all. Nothing means what it once did. The Eucharist is what keeps me returning. It is a solid, physical thing, taken in my hand and broken on my tongue, swallowed and consumed, becoming a part of me. Theologically, it is a sacrament, though I struggle to believe it. Yet I'm holding onto it as a sign of something beyond myself.

Faith has become a hard thing for me, rather than the easy thing I used to take for granted, both as an evangelical and an Episcopalian. I don't talk to God much now. I am out of practice and even when I pray I often feel as if I were talking to myself, or the wall. Yet I want to continue pursuing faith. I am like Jacob at Peniel, wrestling with God.

My Episcopal pastor, Rev. Bonnie Malone, preached a sermon a few weeks ago in which she said that God walks with us in our pain and suffering. The most puzzling, unsettling part of the sermon was what she said about Jesus' appearance in the Upper Room, in the twentieth chapter of John. He tells Thomas to touch his scars. I had read this passage many times, but always concentrating on Thomas' doubt. I hadn't seen the scars: although he had been resurrected, Jesus still had scars.

Books are my life. They are my friends, jesters, consolers, counselors, exhorters, reality instructors and guides. In them I find sustenance and a place to listen to the universal singing of the human soul. I cannot do without them, especially now.

My closest book-bound companion in these days of doubt is Frederick Buechner. His books, especially the four volumes of his autobiography, have been my *vade mecum*. I love the pithy aphoristic wisdom and wit of his "alphabet" books; the peculiar depth of his fiction. I love Buechner's ear for language, his singular psychological insight and keen knowledge of the intersection between the sacred and the profane. He knows the geography of the journey I am on and he is the only Christian writer I can trust right now as a guide and companion through this winter of the spirit.

I copy passages from Buechner's books into my journal, like this one from *Alphabet of Grace*: "Without somehow destroying me in the process, how could God reveal himself in a way that would leave no room for doubt? If there were no room for doubt, there would be no room for me."[3] When I read something like that I know I'm not alone.

For Buechner, God speaks in the mundane and banal even more so than in the flashy and miraculous: "He speaks, I believe, and the words he speaks are incarnate in the flesh of our selves and of our own footsore and sacred journeys."[4] To hear such speech takes listening, and listening with deliberate care. The most significant thing that Buechner has taught me, as he has taught many others, is to listen to my own life.

What this means to me now, in this year following the loss of my faith and the shootings at the abbey, is that I must listen to my depression. I have been depressed for months. It is a genetic inheritance from my father, and though I have not reached the point of clinical depression, the days are darker than they have been. To probe this darkness I must turn and step closer to it, as I would a double of myself, a shadowy *doppelgänger* that crouches on the other side of the window. I want to look it in the face and understand what it can teach me about my own face, my own life. I want to do this but I am afraid it will destroy me.

I haven't surrendered yet. I saw Linda Yeager in Kansas City yesterday and we talked about this. I wondered aloud out exactly what kind of faith I had in the years before this. I don't know and the truth is that I don't need to worry about that anymore. I'm here now. I find that I must continue to choose God, though that means something different to me than it once did. Yet deep inside I still fear that I will have to perform some impossible task in order to prove my faith. Surrender to God seems a leap into living death.

Is this the Dark Night of the Soul? Bonnie Malone has suggested that what I am experiencing is the Dark Night. If she means what John of the Cross means, then I should be glad of it. The Dark Night is how the soul finds its way out of attachment toward the true love of God. If only it weren't so dark, though, and so long. Yet I've decided to teach it: a course next semester on faith and doubt in literature, beginning with Dostoevsky's *The Brothers Karamazov* and including Lagerkvist's *Barrabas* and Wiesel's *Night*. Maybe Hopkins' poetry. Perhaps this is too much like self-flagellation, but teaching for me is like writing, a way of making clear for myself what is now only vague and undefined.

Something happened. Yesterday I was re-reading *The Plague* in preparation for teaching my Existentialism class in the afternoon and got to the horrible, tortured death of the young boy in Part Four and Father Paneloux's response to this in his second sermon. What he says is this: it must be all or nothing. Either we deny that there is a God (in the face of such suffering) or we accept all that God is, which includes the fact that the world is as it is and we won't understand why children must die like the boy did.[5] This either/or put the matter in stark terms for me. Lucid, stark, unambiguous.

That's why Camus, like Buechner, has become another trusted companion of mine, another saint in my pantheon of Winter Saints as I like to think of them. For me, and for old students of mine like Scott Boeckman, Camus' vision is clear about the life lived authentically in the face of human suffering.

"When the throne of God is overturned," Camus writes in *The Rebel*, "the rebel realizes that it is now his own responsibility to create the justice, order, and unity that he sought in vain within his own condition, and in this way to justify the fall of God."[6] For most of his life Albert Camus stood outside the Christian faith. However, in the final decade of his life the French poet of the absurd went through a profound spiritual search. Howard Mumma has recorded in his memoir of the friendship he shared with Camus in Paris during the 1950s. Mumma served as guest minister and preacher at the American Church and Camus came to listen to one of his sermons. They later had lunch together and a unique and valuable friendship was begun.

As Mumma recalls, Camus was even then still searching for something he didn't have: "'I am a disillusioned and exhausted man,'" he confessed to Mumma. "For Camus," Mumma writes, "the mystery of life was a constant struggle, a continuous fight to find truth, forever elusive, yet always calling for him to try once more."[7] Camus did keep trying, even advancing so far in his quest for faith that he asked Mumma to re-baptize him.

I like the idea of always being on the way, of not arriving at any settled *place* of faith. Can the Christian live like this without turning it into an evasion or a fetish? Continue the search, the quest for truth, never turning our eyes away from *reality*. That, it seems to me, is my only way to return. I know now how easy it is for faith to slowly disintegrate within the familiar embrace of structures and rituals and the comfortable assemblies of the pious. Can the Christian stand in solidarity with those who, in all honest integrity at least, cannot believe?

In my deepest self I can't deny God. Nor can I authentically embrace the Void, the Abyss. I cannot go there. Nietzsche, another of my reality instructors, may be right: It may be that I am weak with slavish timidity, craving security and affirmation. But to say "yes" to God out of fear or a need of security is not yet to surrender or submit. Not really. It's more like hedging one's bets, another name for Pascal's wager.

A good deal of religious faith is, I suppose, an inauthentic collapse into soft, comfortable security, but that's not what I am seeking. If I wanted security—or at least the absence of life-changing conflict—I would live my life from impulse to impulse, enjoying the good that life can give me and avoiding as much pain as possible, staying comfortably numb to more pressing questions. That's not hard to do here in America, with enough money, an interesting job, and an adequate health plan. I would even go to church on Sundays.

Faith is a risk, one greater than Nietzsche, the Lutheran preacher's rebellious kid, could comprehend, maybe.

It snowed last night. Winter comes in. I attend church because Peter is teaching Sunday School and Carolyn can't bring him because of her recent spine surgery. But though I am sitting in the pew, I'm no more connected to church-going than I was. I'm going through the motions.

God says that he loves me. Is he a lover I can trust? Is God loving the child in the torturous suffering of the plague? Paneloux sees this love in the figure of the suffering Christ: "No, he, Father Paneloux, would keep faith with the great symbol of all suffering, the tortured body on the Cross; he would stand fast, his back to the wall, and face honestly the terrible problem of a child's agony."[8] God suffers. The thought of this pierces me. But the monks who died in the hallway of the abbey on June 10th were not children, and professed that they were ready to die. That is what becoming a monk is about: a submission of one's will to God, even unto death. Does that make the horror somehow more acceptable?

According to tradition, God experiences death, and the death of the beloved. God does understand, but She is silent, a truth that haunted Camus and haunts me. I feel alone and isolated. Yet I am lifted up by others. I see this most strongly in my family. In the faces of Carolyn and Peter I see God without confusion. If I can hold on to that.

My journey has reached what I hope is a sanctuary in a high country. As an oblate of Conception Abbey I am invited to make Lenten resolutions each year, which are blessed by the Abbot or the Director of Oblates. I hadn't done this for a few years. But this February when the card came in the mail from Father Kenneth, the Oblate Director, I fill it out, listing "practicing silence" and "fasting" as my resolutions. I wasn't going to at first. In fact, I almost threw the envelope in the trash.

The physical act of taking the pen in hand and writing down these resolutions is a step for me, a leap, as Kierkegaard would call it. It seems to me that I have set my face toward Jerusalem, as the Psalmist might put it.

The *Rule of St. Benedict* instructs the monk to make his life "a continuous Lent."[9] That doesn't sound like much fun if we think of Lent as a time of giving up things that we love for seven weeks, like chocolate, computer games, book-buying or beer. St. Benedict was wiser than that. Lent is really about listening without distraction. It is what I seek now.

On Ash Wednesday I eat nothing all day. I've never done this before and I can't believe how difficult it is, especially for an American used to eating more than he needs every day. Other days I eat, but only a limited amount. The hunger that comes from fasting becomes an opportunity for me to listen more attentively to my life and what I value, but on many days it is mostly an annoyance. Through this Lenten country I move slowly, gingerly, into prayer and silence. Mostly silence. Doubts return, as they will, but I decide to pray with them and through them, offering them up to God because there are no real answers of the kind that could completely satisfy me.

Faith seems to be growing in me. Can it do that? In my past I believed that one either had faith or not—was either saved or not. I think I love and trust God more than I did a year ago. I like going to church now more than I did, but it still isn't the same. Perhaps the effort I have to put into faith now is itself the path of faith.

It is March 17th, 2004: St. Patrick's Day. My friend Fr. Patrick Caveglia's name day. I haven't trusted God for two years. I've gone through the motions, attended church, even prayed—but I haven't trusted. It has infected everything, including my marriage. Now I sit in our living room, motionless, heavy with the weight of things done and left undone, words said and unsaid that have caused such pain in others, especially my beloved.

Like the parent of the prodigal, Carolyn comes with sweet, fragrant oil for my forehead, her thumb etching the cross upon the dry parchment of my skin. They call this the *Oleum Infirmorum*, the Oil of the Sick. Mother Bonnie Malone had anointed her for the pain she carries, and now Carolyn anoints me. There is no overt miracle here, no flash of light, no sudden prostration, only a quiet room in a house in a small town in northwest Missouri where a woman who loves me comes with forgiveness and healing in her hands. It's what I need, and what I want. Through her, God touches me. Surrender is sweet, like the sweetest embrace. There are no demands, only the freedom of love. This is what I find at the heart of surrender to God. I couldn't see it before, and I didn't want to believe it.

The ecstasy comes on me in the following days. It is visceral, hormonal, an emotional high like teen-age love. For two weeks my spirit waltzes dizzily with the dancing bears of redemption. It is as if God is throwing a joyous come-as-you-are party where, like me, the host bears the human stain. I feel like I have come full circle, back to the exciting intimacy of my first, youthful, evangelical faith, but tempered with thirty more years of life, and the wisdom to know that feelings about God are not God himself. But it's good to feel good.

Have these passages been steps of faith? Did I really lose my faith, or was it simply another season of the soul, one of necessary doubt. But I know that I did not trust God during this time, and I'm not sure I trusted him for many years before that. I was going through the motions of faith—going to church, praying when I had a mind to, occasionally reading the Bible, and trying to live a decent life. I got "saved" and obsessed about proving the faith, but even then I didn't love God. I had never learned how to love him. It took the monks to show me how.

Chapter Twelve:
The Maze

✤ ✤ ✤

Life moves on; faith unfolds. Seasons pass: Spring follows winter, and summer fades into the cold and wind of autumn. I live out those rich periods when I am practicing spiritual discipline, loving God with the naked fervor and complete surrender of a honeymoon lover, transparent and joy-filled. Then I lose the path. Discipline lapses. Days go by, weeks sometimes, when I don't pray at all. I neglect *lectio divina*. I forget who I am and what I'm about. But I always return. As they will say in the monastery, we fall and get up, fall and get up, fall and get up.

I continue to feel a desire for God, even when it's but a *desire* to desire God, to love God, to surrender to God. Though I made a run at it, I could never make an honest agnostic, much less an atheist. It doesn't seem to be part of me. Going to church has never been bred in me, but the desire or need for God seems to always be there. If this is weakness, it is the needful weakness of a child for its father's arms.

Perhaps it's a gift of grace. Does God give such gifts arbitrarily, or is it according to some plan? I've known many persons who seemed quite comfortable in their lack of a need for God. This was difficult for me to understand when I was a young evangelical. Calvinists have an answer for this, that we are all pre-destined, but I was never a Calvinist. I tend to see faith as everyone's conscious choice—to surrender to God, or to rebel.

When I walked through St. Columba cemetery to be with the monks on the morning of June 10th I was making a choice to love them in spite of my doubts and reservations. When I listen to my life now, years later, I believe that on that awful morning I was called. The call came, clear and dangerous, like the bells I heard on my first morning at the abbey, or, perhaps, like Fr. Conrad's name in the book I bought before I had even heard of the place. I had to take the leap: if I wanted to be with the monks I had to follow the path through the trees. It became a sign for me for entering into the heart of suffering. As Linda Yeager had said to me, I had to suffer because I loved the monks. That's all I knew. It would take years before I came to believe that God was there with me—and with them—on that day, yet it seemed the monks never doubted it.

The philosopher John Caputo has characterized a true love for God as an embracing of the impossible, meaning what we cannot imagine happening in this world, this reality, but which God can do, the "hope against hope . . . in a transforming future."[1] True faith in God blows our doors off. The future is suddenly opened and the impossible is made possible. Our sense of limits, boundaries, and sight is warped out of all expectation. "The religious sense of life," Caputo says, "has to do with exposing oneself to the radical uncertainty and the open-endedness of life."[2] This may be another way of talking about *conversatio*, that Benedictine vow which refers to an openness to change and reformation of one's life as a monk.

Faith is not about arguments or proofs or evidence. Faith seeks understanding, but understanding is not equivalent to faith. Faith is not a once-for-all choice, as I used to believe. One has to continue leaping, stepping out, every day. Like marriage, it's about surrendering to someone we trust enough to surrender to, of coming to the edge of our knowledge and arguments and evidence and proofs and, once there, being asked a question: will you walk with me into the unknown?

At first, the shootings seemed a good opportunity to return my ticket to God, as Ivan Karamazov defiantly declares to his brother Alyosha.[3] To rebel. And there are more than enough horrors each day to challenge faith in a loving God, to affirm what Sartre writes in *Being and Nothingness*, that death is that which "removes all meaning from life."[4] We question why and find no human answer.

To have faith in a loving God in a world such as ours with eyes and hearts wide open is more difficult than not to have faith, despite what the brash atheist shouts in the village square. Especially the faith of the searcher and pilgrim who is uncomfortable with comforting platitudes, skeptical of quick answers, who trusts God yet feels deeply the alienation and bent wrongness of the world. It is a life with the God of the Cross, who is present in suffering and death as he is present in joy and life.

Either life means something, even in the face of the absurdity of death, or it does not. Either there is hope or there is not. Either there is reason for things, or there is not. If not, then those of us who are religious are fooling ourselves, especially when we try to sugar-coat suffering. One of the things I appreciate about the monks is that they do not do this. They are realists about the world. They look at it with open eyes, and they continue to pray and work.

If you walk out of the front doors of the abbey basilica and continue west, across the road, down the hill, you will come upon a stand of small elms planted in an orderly geometric pattern. They are unkept now, running to seed. The trees are all that remains of The Maze. Brother Damian planted it years ago and tended it like he did the rest of the abbey grounds. He built it for the amusement of guests, but I wouldn't be surprised to learn that he had known something of its symbolic significance, remembering how he had once built an elaborate scale model of Notre Dame Cathedral.

Like its cousin the labyrinth, a maze can be a place of bewilderment and confusion. Yet there is an important difference between them. According to Hermann Kern, the labyrinth traditionally signified a structure in which there was but one path to the center. A maze, on the other hand, offered many paths, some leading to dead ends.[5]

Labyrinths are found inscribed in the floors of churches. No one knows why, exactly. Kern suggests that they might represent the labyrinth of the world—of sin and temptation and, ultimately, sanctification, an ordeal of preparation, or a path to God, a substitute for the pilgrimage. Many people have used them this way. Or they may signify initiation: "A walker leaving a labyrinth is not the same person who entered it, but has been born again into a new phase or level of existence; the center is where death and rebirth occur."[6]

In retrospect, life may look like a labyrinth, once we find the center. We see then that there was but one way through. But existentially, as it is lived from day to day, life is a maze, with branching pathways and often unclear choices.

When my son Peter was very young and our family would sometimes take a drive out to the abbey on a Sunday afternoon, he loved to visit Br. Damian's maze. Like all children, he was drawn to the idea of mystery and adventure that it suggested, of the potential of being lost and found. One misty day in September or early October, I think it was, he stepped into the maze with Carolyn and felt suddenly afraid. He reached for his mother's hand.

We want a Northwest Passage, the fabled short-cut through the North American continent to the treasures of the East. We want an easy passage to redemption, to life lived in God's presence: a straight, uncomplicated road through the maze. But there are no short-cuts—no special formulas for prayer or anything else, just as there was no Northwest Passage. We blunder around in the dark night of the soul, lost in our error and confusion, thinking that we've got to find the Way, never realizing that we are already on the way. Where we are going begins always from where we are. God calls us even before we are aware of it. If we come to love him it is because he first loved us and seeks us.

My Protestant, evangelical-formed spirituality was mostly about me and what I got out of a relationship with God: excitement, transcendent happiness, the security-blanket of heaven. What I have learned from the monks and seminarians is that we are in it together and that God calls us out from the self to a labor within a diverse community of others for the sake of the world. We are not alone in this maze we call life. God reaches for us through the lives of other people. By welcoming the stranger, the monks of Conception Abbey extend the welcome and prodigal love of God.

Epilogue

✤ ✤ ✤

It has been over eight years since the shootings. Another autumn settles in with yellowing leaves and colder winds. Another school year. My life once more moves in step with the rhythm of teaching.

My new Freshmen this fall are bright, talkative, and fun to teach. They are earnest, too, about who they are as Catholics and what the Roman Catholic Church should be all about. In other words, they are typical Freshman seminarians. In time, for most of those who remain in the seminary beyond this year and especially the next, formation will turn their zeal toward more pressing matters of inner transformation.

I look at them, remembering all the students who have sat in my classrooms during my years at the seminary. Some here will continue on through seminary and theologate and become priests. I'll read their names in the alumni notices of ordinations in the abbey newsletter, feeling the keen joy of a father reading news of his sons.

But that's in the future. Today they're learning about writing coherent paragraphs. It is the everyday work of academic formation.

In the monastery, work and prayer continues, as it has in Benedictine monasteries for centuries. Abbot Gregory Polan continues to lead the monks of Conception Abbey as a loving father. As happens in any living community, there have been changes here: Novice Andrew Sheller has become Brother Paul—I told him that the Abbot had named him well—and is in graduate school in theology. Father Frowin Reed—brother no longer—is studying for his doctorate in Rome. Father Kenneth Reichert has retired from his job as both Prior and spiritual director and now supervises the monastery infirmary. Fr. Patrick has become the director of the Abbey Center, welcoming the many guests who come to Conception for retreat and conference. He and I still meet and talk about the sometimes puzzling and always interesting paths of life. Chris Anadale has moved on to another job out east and Shalina Stilley has taken his place teaching philosophy. Like Ivan and Alyosha, Dmitri has graduated. I still hear from them, as I do many other of my former students.

As for me, I continue to work out my faith in this intersection of two worlds, Protestant and Catholic. For one who identifies most with an unfinished, imperfect, pilgrim spirituality, a Benedictine abbey, like the Episcopal Church, offers a welcoming sanctuary and challenging workshop for the spiritual life. Here, in this community of Benedictine monks, I find a way of life that runs counter to our self-centered, super-sized, throw-away culture. It is a good place to work, and an even better place to meet God in daily life.

I will let Frederick Buechner have the last word: "Maybe nothing is more important than that we keep track, you and I, of these stories of who we are and where we have come from and the people we have met along the way because it is precisely through these stories in all their particularity . . . that God makes himself known to each of us most powerfully and personally."[1]

Acknowledgements

❖ ❖ ❖

This book was born and fostered within the community of family, friends, and associates who sustain my work as both a teacher and writer. In particular, I want to express my deep gratitude for the friendship and encouragement of Rev. Linda Yeager, who gave me the idea in the first place, and Fr. Patrick Caveglia, friend and spiritual director, whose Benedictine care, wisdom, and practical guidance show forth on nearly every page of this book. Thanks, as well, to Christi Cardenas, friend and guide, for helping to get this project off the ground in its earliest stages and for good counsel over the long haul.

Thanks to those members of the Conception Abbey community who read all or parts of the manuscript and gave me valuable comments on it: Fr. Dan Merz, Fr. Isaac True, Fr. Samuel Russell, and especially Abbot Gregory Polan. A special word of appreciation to the three seminarians who agreed to have their stories included here. Like all of the seminarians I have taught over my years at Conception Seminary College, they continue to inspire me. Thanks to Dan Madden for help on the background and Br. Thomas Sullivan, Abbey Librarian, for his assistance with material from the Conception Abbey Archive. Thanks to Abbot Gregory for permission to quote from the Conception Abbey Necrology.

A writer needs a place to write. Though it's a writer's cliché, my place has been a coffee shop—and one like no other: The Bookstop, in Maryville. Special thanks to its owners and proprietors, Mike and Sheila Phillips, for providing a space for my creative self to romp.

Thanks too, for the early guidance of Giles Anderson and James Quigley, and to John Mark Schuster and the design team at CreateSpace—Jason, Allison, Kayla, Sarah and Ashley—for helping me get this book into print.

Finally, my deepest thanks go to Carolyn, my wife, and Peter, my son. Like the monks, they abide with me on every page.

NOTES

✣ ✣ ✣

Chapter One: Signs
1. Walker Percy, "Morality and Religion," in *Signposts in a Strange Land*, edited by Patrick Samway (New York: Farrar, Straus and Giroux, 1991), 314.
2. Frederick Buechner, *The Sacred Journey* (San Francisco: Harper & Row, 1982), 77.

Chapter Two: Fathers and Sons
1. Ian Vandewalker, "Nefarious Nietzsche," *Philosophical Powers*, http://homepages.nyu.edu/~iav202/powers/nietzsche.html.
2. Fyodor Dostoevski, *The Brothers Karamazov*, translated by Richard Pevear and Larissa Volokhonsky (New York: Farrar, Straus and Giroux, 2002).

Chapter Three: Catholics
1. John Paul II, *I Will Give You Shepherds* [Pastores Dabo Vobis] (Washington, D.C.: United States Catholic Conference, 1992), 113.
2. Bob Dylan, *Chronicles: Volume One* (New York: Simon & Schuster, 2004), 9.
3. Allan Sherman, "Hello Muddah, Hello Faddah (A Letter from Camp)," *Rhino High-Five: Allan Sherman*, audio download from iTunes, 2005 Rhino Entertainment.
4. Walter Isaacson, *Einstein: His Life and Universe* (New York: Simon & Schuster, 2007), 67.

Chapter Four: Telling Stories
1. Greg Carl, unpublished haiku.
2. Tim O'Brien, "How to Tell a True War Story," in *The Things They Carried* (New York: Broadway Books, 1998), 67–85.
3. Andrew Greeley, "Why I'm Still a Catholic," *Andrew M. Greeley: Author, Priest, Sociologist*, http://www.agreeley.com/articles/why.html.

Chapter Five: Communion
1. Soren Kierkegaard, *The Sickness Unto Death: A Christian Psychological Exposition for Upbuilding and Awakening* (Princeton: Princeton University Press, 1980), 13.

Chapter Six: Brothers in Black
1. Jean-Paul Sartre, *No Exit*, in *No Exit, and Three Other Plays*, translated by Stuart Gilbert (New York: Vintage, 1989), 45.
2. Saint Benedict, *The Rule of St. Benedict: In Latin and English with Notes*, edited by Timothy Fry, OSB, et al. (Collegeville, MN: The Liturgical Press, 1980), 267.

3. Saint Benedict, 157.
4. *Conception Abbey Necrology*, Conception Abbey Archives.
5. Ibid.

Chapter Eight: Euthyphro
1. Plato, *Euthyphro*, in *The Collected Dialogues*, edited by Edith Hamilton and Huntington Cairns, translated by Lane Cooper (Princeton: Princeton University Press, 1961), 173.
2. Martin Heidegger, *An Introduction to Metaphysics*, translated by Ralph Manheim (New Haven: Yale University Press, 1959), 11.

Chapter Nine: The Woods
1. John Updike, *In the Beauty of the Lilies* (New York: Ballantine Books, 1996), 5.
2. Paul Tillich, *The Dynamics of Faith* (New York: Harper & Brothers, 1957), 1–8.
3. Tillich, 18.

Chapter Ten: The Stranger
1. Fr. Gregory Polan, OSB, "Mass of Christian Burial for Father Philip Schuster, OSB, and Brother Damian Larson, OSB," Conception Abbey, http://www.conceptionabbey.org/ June102002/homily061402.htm.

Chapter Eleven: Passages
1. William Least Heat Moon, *Blue Highways: A Journey Into America* (Boston: Atlantic Monthly Press/Little, Brown, 1982), 215.
2. T. S. Eliot, *Ash Wednesday*, in *The Complete Poems and Plays 1909–1950*, 60–67 (New York: Harcourt, Brace & World, 1971), 65.

3. Frederick Buechner, *The Alphabet of Grace* (New York: Harper & Row, 1970), 47.
4. Buechner, *The Sacred Journey* (San Francisco: Harper & Row, 1982), 77.
5. Albert Camus, *The Plague*, translated by Stuart Gilbert (New York: Vintage, 1991), 222–28.
6. Albert Camus, *The Rebel: An Essay on Man in Revolt*, translated by Anthony Bower (New York: Vintage, 1956), 25.
7. Howard Mumma, *Albert Camus and the Minister* (Brewster, MA: Paraclete Press, 2000), 14, 63.
8. Camus, *The Plague*, 224.
9. Saint Benedict, 253.

Chapter Twelve: The Maze
1. John Caputo, *On Religion* (London: Routledge, 2001), 11.
2. Caputo, 14.
3. Fyodor Dostoevsky, *The Brothers Karamazov*. Trans Richard Pevear and Larissa Volokhonsky (New York: Farrar, Straus and Giroux, 2002), 245.
4. Jean-Paul Sartre, *Being and Nothingness*, translated by Hazel E. Barnes (New York: Pocket Books, 1992), 690.
5. Hermann Kern, *Through the Labyrinth: Designs and Meanings over 5,000 Years*, translated by Abigail Clay (Munich: Prestel Verlag, 2000), 23.
6. Kern, 30.

Epilogue
1. Frederick Buechner, *Telling Secrets* (San Francisco: HarperSanFrancisco, 1991), 30.

Made in the USA
Charleston, SC
08 August 2011